Sugar-Free Diabetic-Friendly

20 Minute Healthy Air Fryer

Cookbook for Two

75 Healthy Dinners +

20 Sweet Indulgence Desserts+

30 Tasty Bites and Savory Snacklets

Cristina Turingray

Table of Content

Table of Content

Table of Content

IV. HEALTHY SEAFOOD AND VEGETARIAN DINNER RECIPES

V. HEALTHY PIZZAS AND CREPES

Table of Content

VI. SWEET INDULGENCE DESSERTS: SUGAR-FREE AND DIABETIC-FRIENDLY

What to Expect from This Cookbook

Welcome to your new kitchen companion, crafted to transform how you cook for two. Whether you're a busy professional, a couple looking to inject some creativity into your meals, or managing dietary needs like diabetes, this cookbook is designed with you in mind. Here's what you can expect:

EFFICIENCY AND SIMPLICITY:
Each recipe in this book is structured to take 20 minutes or less, using your air fryer to its full potential. We know your time is precious, so we've made quick, healthy eating a straightforward and stress-free experience.

HEALTH-FOCUSED RECIPES:
With 75 dinner and 20 dessert recipes, you'll find dishes that not only tantalize your taste buds but also support your health goals. Each recipe is developed to be rich in nutrients, low in unhealthy fats, and suitable for a diabetic diet, focusing on natural ingredients and balanced macros.

TAILORED FOR TWO:
Cooking for two can be a challenge, with recipes often catering to larger families. We've carefully portioned each recipe to suit you and your partner, avoiding unnecessary leftovers and minimizing waste.

SUGAR-FREE AND DIABETIC-FRIENDLY DESSERTS:
Indulge without guilt with our 20 dessert recipes, all sugar-free and suitable for those managing diabetes. These desserts use alternative sweeteners and diabetes-friendly ingredients to ensure you can enjoy sweet treats responsibly.

PRACTICAL TIPS AND TRICKS:
Beyond recipes, gain insights into getting the most out of your air fryer with tips on maintenance, optimal settings for different dishes, and quick fixes to common issues. Educational Insights: Learn about the principles of healthy eating, the importance of dietary fiber and protein, and how to effectively manage carbohydrates in your diet, especially pertinent for blood sugar control. Navigational Tools: With a detailed index and glossary, you can quickly find the information or recipe you need and understand the nutritional terms that are vital for a healthy lifestyle. This cookbook is more than just a collection of recipes—it's a guide to healthier, more enjoyable cooking and eating for two, making every meal an opportunity to nourish both body and relationship.

Why an Air Fryer?

Welcome to a culinary adventure designed for two, where the whirl of an air fryer fan brings not just convenience but a revolution in your kitchen. You are about to discover how this marvelous machine transforms cooking from a mundane task to a thrilling journey of taste and health.

In the fast-paced world we live in, making time to prepare healthy meals can often seem like a herculean task, especially when traditional cooking methods demand more than we can spare. Enter the air fryer—a modern kitchen miracle that promises to reclaim your time and health.

With the ability to grill, bake, and roast, an air fryer isn't just another kitchen gadget; it's your partner in the quest for healthier eating.

Imagine cutting down the fat in your meals by up to 80% without sacrificing flavor. Imagine crispy textures and succulent flavors, all achieved with minimal oil. This isn't just cooking; it's an upgrade to your diet and lifestyle, streamlined through technology. The air fryer offers a simple truth: healthy cooking doesn't have to be a luxury or a marathon. It can be quick, easy, and absolutely delicious.

From golden brown fries to juicy chicken breasts, the possibilities are endless. The air fryer is a versatile tool that can transform your favorite indulgent treats into guilt-free delights. It's not just about convenience; it's about making healthier choices accessible to everyone, regardless of their cooking skill level. Moreover, cleaning up after cooking with an air fryer is a breeze. Most models come with dishwasher-safe components, meaning you spend less time scrubbing pots and pans and more time savoring your meals.

Understanding Your Air Fryer

HOW IT WORKS:
THE INTRICATE DANCE OF HEAT AND AIR

THE ALCHEMY OF RAPID AIR TECHNOLOGY:

At the heart of the air fryer's wizardry lies the Rapid Air Technology. Think of it as a miniature tempest in a metal box, where heat sourced from a close-quartered element is whipped into a frenzy by a high-powered fan. This creates a cyclone of superheated air that envelops the food, crisping the exterior to a perfect golden hue while locking moisture within. The result? Dishes that are sumptuously tender on the inside and delightfully crisp on the outside.

ELEVATED COOKING SURFACES:

The secret to this culinary enchantment is the air fryer's basket design, where food rests on a grate elevated above the chamber floor. This arrangement allows the heated air to circulate freely around the food, ensuring every morsel is evenly cooked. Whether it's a succulent piece of meat or tender vegetables, each comes out with a perfectly crisped exterior and a juicy interior.

VERSATILE COOKING ENCLOSURES:

For those dishes that thrive in a gentler environment—where crusts are unwelcome and moisture is paramount—the air fryer shows its flexible charm. Wrapping ingredients in foil or placing them in a baking sleeve transforms the air fryer into a gentle baker. These encased morsels steam in their own juices, emerging moist and tender. You can even place these foil-wrapped treasures atop a steak, letting them cook in unison, marrying flavors in a harmonious feast ready in moments.

SILICONE ACCESSORIES AND EVEN BAKING:

Further enhancing its versatility, the air fryer welcomes an array of silicone accessories, each designed to perfect your culinary creations. These tools ensure even cooking and easy handling. Imagine placing raw croissants into the fryer and, within 25 minutes, witnessing them puff into golden, evenly baked pastries, their aroma wafting through your kitchen like a promise of a Parisian morning.

Essential Air Frying Techniques:
Must-Read Tips for Every Cook

1. TEMPERATURE TIPS FOR OPTIMAL COOKING
The higher the temperature, the drier and crispier your food will become when cooked in an air fryer. For a crispy crust, set the temperature to 390°F (200°C). If you are concerned about food burning on the top, lower the temperature. For instance, broccoli florets can dry out very quickly and for perfectly crispy thin sweet potato chips, the ideal temperature is 300°F (150°C).

2. ACHIEVING SOFTNESS WITHOUT CRISPINESS
If you prefer vegetables that are soft but not crispy, consider baking them in foil or a cooking sleeve. This method allows vegetables to steam within their enclosure and can be placed directly on top of other foods in the air fryer.

3. UTILIZING SILICONE MOLDS
Use thin silicone molds for baking dishes that require more baking than grilling, and for foods prepared in sauce. These molds help distribute heat evenly, ensuring your food cooks properly without direct exposure to intense heat.

4. EXPANDING COOKING CAPACITY
Consider purchasing a skewer rack for air fryers, which effectively adds a second layer to your cooking space. This setup is ideal for cooking multiple items at once and is particularly great for kebabs, which always turn out well in an air fryer.

5. SPECIALTY COOKING SURFACES
A flat, round silicone mat can be invaluable for cooking pizza in the air fryer. It can also be used along with a skewer rack for making bruschetta, allowing for even cooking and easy handling.

6. AVOID OVERCROWDING:
Like a battalion that needs room to maneuver, ensure that the air fryer's basket is not overly crowded. This space allows for the free circulation of hot air, which is essential for achieving evenly cooked fare.

Modes and Settings

In the versatile world of air fryers, the magic unfolds through a variety of settings that cater to the myriad culinary endeavors of any kitchen bard. Understanding the modes and settings of your air fryer is akin to mastering the strings of a lute, where each strum brings forth a new melody, or in our case, a dish crafted to perfection. Let's delve into these settings, tailored to suit both robust dinners and delicate desserts.

TEMPERATURE MASTERY:

Your air fryer's ability to precisely control temperature is its most crucial feature. For heartier dinner fare, such as crispy chicken thighs or roasted root vegetables, higher temperatures are paramount. These settings allow the exterior of your food to develop a rich, caramelized crust while preserving moist tenderness within. Conversely, when you venture into the sweet territory of desserts, a milder heat setting is often your ally. Gentle warmth is sufficient to puff pastry shells or to bake fruit crumbles without scorching delicate sugars.

TIMER CONTROL:

Every setting is complemented by a timer, a faithful squire that ensures no dish is left to the perils of overcooking. For dinners, where timing is crucial to achieving that perfect sear or roast, the timer can be set to the precise minute. Desserts often require a more delicate hand, and thus, a keen eye on the countdown, ensuring that your sweet creations emerge at the peak of perfection.

CUSTOM MODES:

Many air fryers come equipped with pre-programmed settings tailored to specific dishes. These might include modes for baking, which lower the fan speed to avoid unsettling light batters, or grilling settings, which maximize heat from the top element to mimic the radiant heat of a grill. Exploring these can streamline your cooking process, making the preparation of both dinners and desserts a more intuitive and effortless endeavor.

PREHEAT FUNCTION:

Like the prelude to a grand performance, preheating your air fryer ensures that it is ready to perform at its best from the moment ingredients enter its chamber. This is especially important for recipes requiring precise cooking environments from the start, be it a quick-searing steak or a batch of mini quiches.

Air Fryer Temperature and Time Guide
for Different Dishes

1. MEATS:

Chicken: For juicy, tender chicken with a crisp exterior, set your air fryer to 360°F (180°C) and cook for about 15-25 minutes, depending on the size of the pieces. If you're cooking chicken wings or drumsticks, they may need less time, approximately 12-20 minutes.

Beef: Steaks are best cooked at a higher temperature for a shorter time to replicate the high heat of grilling. Set the air fryer to 390°F (200°C) and cook a 1-inch steak for about 8-10 minutes for medium-rare.

Pork: Pork chops with a slight thickness will cook beautifully at 375°F (190°C) for about 12-15 minutes, turning halfway through to ensure even cooking.

2. SEAFOOD:

Fish Fillets: Delicate items like fish fillets cook quickly. Set the air fryer to 360°F (180°C) and cook for 10-12 minutes. This is sufficient to cook the fish through without drying it out.

Shrimp: Shrimp cooks even faster and should be air fried at 360°F (180°C) for 6-8 minutes. It's perfect for a quick, healthy dinner.

3. VEGETABLES:

Root Vegetables: Carrots, potatoes, and beets, diced into small pieces, cook best at 380°F (190°C) for about 15-20 minutes. Stir halfway through cooking for even results.

Leafy Greens: Vegetables like kale or spinach for chips should be cooked at 360°F (180°C) for just 5-7 minutes. It's a quick way to make a crispy, healthy snack.

4.SNACKS:

French Fries: To achieve the perfect crispy texture, cut potatoes into thin strips and soak them in water for a few hours to remove excess starch. Pat them dry, season with salt and your favorite spices, and cook at 380°F (190°C) for 15-20 minutes.

Mozzarella Sticks: These cheesy delights can be cooked at 390°F (200°C) for 6-8 minutes. Be sure to freeze them for at least 30 minutes before air frying to prevent the cheese from oozing out too quickly.

5.DESSERTS:

Cakes and Muffins: These need a moderate temperature to rise without burning. Bake at 325°F (165°C) for about 15-20 minutes.

Cookies: Set the air fryer to 350°F (180°C) and bake for just 5-8 minutes depending on the cookie size and dough type.

Apple Chips: Thinly slice apples and sprinkle with a bit of cinnamon. Air fry at 350°F (175°C) for 10-12 minutes, flipping halfway through.

Quick Tips and Tricks

PREPARATION HACKS: TIME-SAVING TIPS SPECIFICALLY FOR AIR FRYER USE

Mastering the air fryer can revolutionize your kitchen routine with efficiency and flair. Here are some clever hacks to streamline your cooking process, ensuring that even the busiest days can include a healthy, homemade meal:

- **PREHEAT TO PERFECTION:**
 Just like a traditional oven, preheating your air fryer can significantly improve cooking outcomes. Taking just a few minutes to preheat ensures that foods start cooking immediately and evenly, perfect for achieving that desirable crispy texture.

- **BATCH IT UP:**
 For efficiency, cook ingredients in batches that can be mixed and matched throughout the week. For example, roast a variety of vegetables or cook multiple chicken breasts at once. Store them properly, and you'll have versatile components ready to toss into quick salads, wraps, or reheated for a rapid re-run.

- **SHAKE OR TOSS MID-COOK:**
 To avoid having to flip items individually, give the basket a quick shake or toss midway through cooking. This simple move helps achieve an even crispness on all sides of your food, mimicking the effect of flipping without the hassle.

- **USE PARCHMENT ROUNDS:**
 Invest in perforated parchment rounds designed for air fryers. These not only help in keeping the basket clean but also prevent smaller or delicate items from sticking or falling through the basket's holes.

- **ACCESSORIZE:**
 Maximize your air fryer's potential with accessories like racks or skewers, which allow you to double the cooking surface or prepare multiple meal components at once—think steak on one level and veggies on another.

Care and Maintenance:
Preserving the Valor of Your Air

FRYER

In the grand tapestry of your kitchen, your air fryer stands as a steadfast sentinel, guarding the realms of healthy cuisine. To ensure that it continues to serve valiantly, certain protocols must be followed—none more critical than the triad of care: safeguarding from falls, timely cleansing, and vigilance for error messages.

GUARD AGAINST FALLS: THE FIRST PRECAUTION

The initial, and perhaps most crucial, act of maintenance is to protect your air fryer from the ignominy of a fall. Much like a knight protects his shield from dents and scratches, you must ensure your appliance is placed securely on the countertop. A fall could be disastrous, potentially shattering its glass or damaging its internal components, rendering it as forlorn as a knight without armor.

TIMELY CLEANING: THE RITUAL OF READINESS

After each culinary quest, allow your air fryer to cool to the touch, which marks the perfect time to begin the cleaning ritual. Regular cleaning not only maintains the noble appearance of your appliance but also prevents the build-up of food particles and grease, which can impair its performance over time. Dismantle the removable parts—basket, tray, and pan—and cleanse them in the warm, soapy waters of the kitchen sink. For the interior and the heating element—a gentle wipe with a damp cloth should suffice to keep the machine in prime condition.

Deep Cleaning: Engage periodically in a deep cleaning, especially after a series of intensive uses. For stubborn stains or odors, employ a gentle paste made of baking soda and water, which acts as a mild abrasive to cleanse without harm.

HEED THE HERALD OF ERROR MESSAGES: THE SIGNS OF THE AIR FRYER

Modern air fryers, much like the heralds of old, come equipped with digital displays that issue forth error messages should trouble arise. These messages are crucial; they are the early warnings of potential maladies within your appliance. Attend them immediately, consulting the user manual—a tome of knowledge—for guidance on remedies. This vigilance will prevent minor issues from festering into critical failures, ensuring that your air fryer remains a reliable companion.

The Basics of Healthy Eating

The Basics of Healthy Eating

NUTRITIONAL FOUNDATIONS: A BALANCING ACT FOR WELLNESS

In the grand narrative of health and nourishment, the concept of a balanced diet emerges as the cornerstone. To embark upon a journey of sustained wellness, particularly for those navigating the complexities of diabetes, is to understand the alchemy of combining ingredients not only for their flavor but also for their fortifying properties.

Harmony of Nutrients: A balanced diet, like a well-tuned orchestra, requires the harmonious integration of various nutrients—carbohydrates, proteins, fats, vitamins, and minerals. Each plays a unique role: carbohydrates provide the fuel, proteins build and repair tissues, fats cushion and insulate, vitamins guide processes, and minerals act as building blocks.

CARBOHYDRATES WITH CAUTION:

In the world of diabetes management, carbohydrates take center stage, but not all are created equal. The focus shifts to those that are complex and fiber-rich—think whole grains, legumes, and dense vegetables. These champions of the dietary realm break down slowly, releasing glucose steadily, thus maintaining the even keel of blood sugar levels, much like a steady hand guiding a ship through stormy seas.

PROTEINS:

The Steadfast Allies: Proteins in a diabetic-friendly diet are akin to loyal knights upholding the body's structure and function. Sources like lean meats, fish, tofu, and legumes not only support bodily repairs but also contribute to a feeling of fullness, preventing the common foe of overeating.

FATS:

The Misunderstood Elementals: Once vilified, fats have regained their place at the table, albeit with a focus on those that heal rather than harm. Monounsaturated and polyunsaturated fats—found in avocados, nuts, seeds, and fish—work like the subtle magics that bolster health, improving blood cholesterol levels and stabilizing heart rhythms.

FIBER:

The Great Regulator: Fiber, especially soluble fiber, acts much like the wise advisor in tales of old, regulating digestion and blood sugar levels. By incorporating a wealth of fruits, vegetables, and whole grains into one's diet, one ensures that the digestive tract works not as a foe to be battled but as a companion in the quest for health.

The Basics of Healthy Eating

THE PLATE METHOD:

A Visual Guide for Balance: Imagine your plate as a map of a kingdom, where each territory must be proportioned wisely. Half the plate should be adorned with vegetables and fruits, a quarter with lean proteins, and the remaining quarter with wholesome grains or starchy vegetables. This visual guide helps in crafting meals that are not only balanced but also kingdoms of flavor and nutrition.

By embracing these principles, one crafts a diet that is less about restriction and more about thoughtful selection, a strategy that not only manages diabetes effectively but also enhances overall vitality. This approach to eating is not merely a daily routine but an artful way to live, ensuring each meal brings joy and health in equal measure.

ROLE OF CARBOHYDRATES: THE DELICATE DANCE OF SUGAR AND HEALTH

In the vast tapestry of nutrition, carbohydrates stand as a crucial, albeit complex, thread, woven intricately into the fabric of our daily sustenance. Understanding carbohydrates is akin to learning the language of your body's energy system—knowing it well allows you to better manage its impact, especially on blood sugar levels.

THE DUAL NATURE OF CARBOHYDRATES:

Carbohydrates, the primary fuel for the body, come in two main forms—simple and complex. Simple carbohydrates are like fleeting whispers in a bustling market, quick to enter the bloodstream and just as swift in their departure, causing abrupt peaks and troughs in blood sugar levels. Found in sugars, such as those in honey, fruits, and sweets, they provide instant energy but little sustenance.

Complex carbohydrates, on the other hand, are the narrators of a slow, unfolding story. They are found in foods like whole grains, legumes, and fibrous vegetables. Their structure requires time to break down, resulting in a gradual, more stable release of glucose into the bloodstream. This steadiness helps maintain energy levels and keeps hunger at bay, akin to a well-paced plot that keeps a reader engaged without overwhelming them.

The Basics of Healthy Eating

FIBER: THE MODERATOR:

Integral to the tale of carbohydrates is fiber, a component that does not break down into glucose. Instead, it passes through the body undigested, aiding digestive health and moderating the absorption of sugar. Soluble fiber, in particular, acts much like a diplomatic envoy in a complex political saga—it can slow down the absorption of sugar and lower blood glucose levels, providing a stabilizing influence on the often volatile sugar levels in the body.

GLYCEMIC INDEX: THE CHARACTER GAUGE OF CARBOHYDRATES:

Just as characters in a story are assessed by their depth and complexity, carbohydrates are evaluated by their glycemic index (GI)—a measure of how quickly foods containing carbohydrates raise blood sugar levels. Foods with a high GI are rapid influencers—they cause blood sugar levels to spike. Low GI foods, like your steadfast protagonists, induce a slow and steady rise in blood sugar, offering a more sustained form of energy and minimal disruption to the body's metabolic harmony.

STRATEGIC EATING:

For those managing diabetes or seeking to stabilize their energy levels, the strategy lies in choosing carbohydrates wisely. Opting for low to moderate GI foods, balancing carbohydrate intake with fiber, proteins, and healthy fats, and understanding portion sizes can transform the simple act of eating into a finely tuned art. This approach not only keeps blood sugar levels in check but also supports overall health, allowing one to navigate their day with the same precision and grace as a skilled captain sailing through uncharted waters.

Ingredient Swaps: Recommendations for Sugar Substitutes

and Healthy Alternatives for Common Ingredients

ADAPTING RECIPES FOR HEALTH CAN BE BOTH CREATIVE AND SATISFYING. HERE ARE SOME SMART SWAPS TO KEEP YOUR MEALS BOTH DELICIOUS AND NUTRITIOUS:

- **FOR SUGAR:**

Opt for natural sweeteners like stevia, erythritol, or monk fruit sweetener in place of sugar. These alternatives offer the sweetness without impacting blood sugar levels dramatically, making them ideal for diabetic-friendly recipes or for anyone reducing their sugar intake.

- **FOR FLOUR:**

Replace white flour with almond or coconut flour for a lower-carbohydrate, higher-fiber alternative. These flours are not only gluten-free but also add a rich, nutty flavor to baked goods and help keep you fuller longer.

- **FOR OILS AND FATS:**

When you do need to use oil, choose high-smoke-point oils like avocado or extra light olive oil, which are healthier and safer at the high temperatures generated by air fryers. Alternatively, for many recipes, you can reduce the amount of oil significantly or even omit it altogether due to the air fryer's efficient cooking method.

- **FOR CREAM:**

In recipes calling for cream, try using full-fat Greek yogurt or coconut cream as a substitute. These provide the creaminess and richness without the added heaviness of cream, plus they contribute additional protein or healthy fats.

- **FOR MEATS:**

Swap out higher-fat meats for leaner cuts or use plant-based proteins like tofu or tempeh. These substitutions not only reduce fat intake but also encourage a varied diet, introducing new textures and flavors to your dishes.

Incorporating these tips and swaps into your air fryer cooking routine can transform the way you approach meal preparation, making it quicker, healthier, and more enjoyable. Each small change or hack is a step towards a healthier lifestyle, proving that convenience and health can indeed go hand in hand.

Healthy Meat Dinner Recipes

Steak with Asparagus, Mushrooms, and Sweet Potato Straws

SERVINGS: 2   COOKING TIME: 20 MIN   CALORIES: 450

Ingredients

- Steaks (2 steaks,
  about 6 oz or 170 g each)
- Asparagus (1 bunch, ends trimmed)
- Mushrooms (8 oz or 225 g, sliced)
- Sweet potato (1 large, peeled and cut
  into thin straws, optional)
  (You can also use any frozen
  vegetable mix you like to wrap it in
  the foil and cook with steak)
- Olive oil or another high-smoke-
  point oil
  (2 tablespoons or 30 mL)
- Salt and pepper, to taste
- Fresh herbs (such as rosemary or
  thyme), finely chopped, for garnish

This dish is a wonderful symphony of textures and flavors, perfect when you want a meal that feels indulgent but is straightforward to prepare. The steaks are succulent and perfectly seasoned, the vegetables retain all their natural sweetness and bite. Not only is this meal visually impressive, but it's also packed with nutrients and is low in calories.

Directions

1. Preparation: If using sweet potatoes, soak the straws in water for about 20 minutes to remove excess starch, which helps them crisp up when cooked.

2. Pat the steaks dry with paper towels and season generously with salt and pepper.

3. Prepare the Vegetables: Tear off a large piece of aluminum foil, enough to comfortably wrap the asparagus and mushrooms together.

4. Place the asparagus and mushrooms in the center of the foil, drizzle with olive oil, and season with salt, pepper, and a sprinkle of fresh herbs. Fold the foil over the vegetables to create a sealed packet.

5. Cook the Sweet Potato Straws: Drain the sweet potato straws and pat them dry. Toss them lightly with oil and a pinch of salt. Spread them around the edges of the air fryer basket or add them to the foil to other vegetables.

6. Cooking: Place the steaks in the center of the air fryer basket. Put the foil packet on top of the steaks to allow the heat from the bottom to cook the steak while the vegetables steam in their juices above.

7. Set the air fryer to 400°F (204°C) and cook for about 20 minutes, or until the steak reaches your desired level of doneness and the vegetables are tender.

21

Tangy Lemon Garlic Chicken with Brussels Sprouts

SERVINGS: 2   COOKING TIME: 20 MIN   CALORIES: 455

Ingredients

For the chicken:
- 2 chicken breasts
(500 grams or 1.1 lbs)
- 1 tablespoon olive oil (14 grams)
- 1 lemon, juiced
(2 tablespoons or 30 milliliters)
- 3 cloves garlic, minced (9 grams)
- Salt and pepper to taste (a pinch of each)

For the Brussels sprouts:
- 1.5 cups Brussels sprouts, cut in half
(230 grams)
- 1 tablespoon olive oil (14 grams)
- Salt and pepper to taste (a pinch of each)

Directions

1. Preheat your air fryer to 400°F (200°C).
2. In a bowl, mix together the olive oil, lemon juice, minced garlic, salt, and pepper. Add the chicken breasts, making sure they are well coated.
3. Place the marinated chicken breasts in the air fryer's basket.
4. In another bowl, toss the Brussels sprouts with olive oil, salt, and pepper.
5. Arrange the Brussels sprouts around the chicken in the air fryer's basket.
6. Cook for about 20 minutes, or until the chicken is fully cooked and the Brussels sprouts are brown and crispy.
7. Let the chicken rest for a few minutes before serving.

The lemon and garlic marinade tenderizes the chicken while adding a burst of tangy and aromatic notes. Brussels sprouts, on the other hand, offer a serving of greens that's high on fiber and antioxidants, adding a delightful crunch and earthiness to the meal. A fresh lemon wedge on the side always does wonders, releasing a squirt of brightness to elevate the dish.

Did you know that Brussels sprouts are a member of the Gemmifera Group of cabbages and are, indeed, mini-cabbages in their own right? No wonder they're so packed with nutrients! Now you can enjoy your dinner without any guilt but lots of flavor.

Honey Mustard Beef with Broccoli Florets and Sweet Potato

SERVINGS: 2   COOKING TIME: 20 MIN   CALORIES: 350

Ingredients

- 1 pound of lean sirloin steak (450 grams)
- 2 tablespoons of honey mustard (30 ml)
- Salt and pepper to taste
- 2 cups broccoli florets (about 200 grams)
- 1 large sweet potato, peeled and cut into wedges (about 200 grams)
- 1 tablespoon olive oil (15 ml)
- 2 cloves of garlic, minced

ADD TASTY BITES

MINI STUFFED PEPPERS:
Stuff mini bell peppers with a mix of cream cheese, shredded cheddar, and finely chopped onions. Air fry at 360°F (182°C) for about 10 minutes or until the peppers are soft and the cheese is melted. Perfect for a savory party snack

Directions

1. Season the sirloin steak with salt, pepper, and honey mustard. Let it sit for a while to marinate.
2. Meanwhile, in a bowl, toss broccoli florets and sweet potato wedges with olive oil and minced garlic to coat evenly.
3. Place the steak in the basket of the air fryer first, ensuring it lays flat.
4. Next, arrange the broccoli and sweet potato wedges evenly around the steak if you want them crunchy. If you prefer vegetables juicy, wrap all the vegetables in aluminum foil.
5. Set the air fryer to 400°F (200°C) and cook for approximately 15-18 minutes for medium doneness on the steak and until the vegetables are slightly browned and tender.
6. Check the doneness of your steak and vegetables, extending the cooking time if necessary.
7. Allow the steak to rest for a minute or two before slicing.

With its lean protein, nutrient-rich broccoli, and fiber-packed sweet potato, this dish is wholesome, balanced, and full of flavor. The honey mustard adds a tangy twist to the beef that complements the earthy vegetables perfectly. Plus, cooking it in an air fryer ensures a quick and healthy meal that's easy to make, and easier to enjoy. Did you know lean beef is not only a great source of protein but also packed with iron? So go ahead, savor every bite knowing it's not just delicious, but also nutritious! This meal could easily become a regular in your quick healthy dinner menu.

Mediterranean Chicken Skewers

SERVINGS: 2   COOKING TIME: 20 MIN   CALORIES: 350

Ingredients

- 2 boneless, skinless chicken breasts, cut into cubes
- 1/2 cup olive oil
- Juice of 1 lemon
- 3 cloves garlic, minced
- 1 tbsp dried oregano
- Salt and pepper, to taste
- 1 bell pepper, cut into pieces
- 1 red onion, cut into wedges
- Cherry tomatoes
- Wooden or metal skewers

Directions

1. In a bowl, whisk together olive oil, lemon juice, minced garlic, oregano, salt, and pepper.
2. Add the chicken cubes to the marinade and let sit in the refrigerator for at least 2 hours, or overnight for best results.
3. Preheat your air fryer to 360°F (182°C).
4. Thread the marinated chicken, bell pepper, onion, and cherry tomatoes onto the skewers.
5. Place the skewers in the air fryer basket and cook for 12-15 minutes, turning halfway through, until the chicken is thoroughly cooked and vegetables are tender.
6. Serve with a side of tzatziki sauce and pita bread.

These Mediterranean Chicken Skewers are not only a feast for the eyes with their vibrant colors but also a perfect blend of protein and fiber, making them a nutritious option for any meal. The history of skewered and grilled meat dishes dates back thousands of years, with evidence suggesting that ancient Egyptians and Greeks enjoyed similar cooking methods. The word "kebab" itself likely originated from Arabic or Persian languages, and such dishes are a staple in cuisines around the Mediterranean and Middle East. This cooking style is beloved for its simplicity and the deep flavors it can impart, especially when herbs and marinades are used to enhance the natural tastes of the ingredients.

Succulent Chicken Teriyaki with Crunchy Broccoli and Carrots

SERVINGS: 2   COOKING TIME: 20 MIN   CALORIES: 360

Ingredients

- 2 boneless chicken breasts (approximately 1 lb or 450 grams)
- 2 tablespoons of teriyaki sauce (30 mL)
- 1 tablespoon of honey (15 mL)
- 1 tablespoon of sesame seeds (15 mL)
- 2 cups of fresh broccoli florets (240 gr)
- 2 cups of sliced carrots (300 grams)
(You can also use any frozen vegetable mix you prefer; simply wrap it in foil and cook on the top of main dish.)
- 3 tablespoons of olive oil (45 mL)
- Salt and black pepper to taste

ADD SAVORY SNACKLETS

SWEET POTATO TOTS:
Grate sweet potatoes, squeeze out the excess moisture, and mix with a little cornstarch, salt, and pepper. Form into small tots and air fry at 400°F (204°C) for about 15 minutes, turning halfway through. Dip them in your favorite sauce for a sweet and savory treat.

Directions

1. Season both sides of the chicken breasts with salt and pepper.
2. Mix the teriyaki sauce and honey in a bowl, then coat the chicken breasts evenly in the mixture, ensuring both sides are well covered.
3. Place the coated chicken breasts at the bottom of the air fryer.
4. In a separate bowl, toss the broccoli florets and sliced carrots in olive oil, salt, and pepper.
5. Carefully arrange the seasoned vegetables into the air fryer, spreading them evenly over the top of the chicken breasts.
6. Set the air fryer to cook at 400°F (200°C) for 10 minutes.
7. After the 10 minutes, carefully turn the chicken breasts over and continue cooking for another 8 minutes.
8. To finish, sprinkle the dish with sesame seeds, then cook for a final 2 minutes to lightly toast the seeds.
9. Remove the dish from the air fryer and let it sit for a few minutes before serving.

Chicken teriyaki is a beloved Japanese dish that's easy to make and packed with protein. The teriyaki sauce and honey give the chicken a sweet and savory glaze, perfectly balanced by the sesame seeds' nutty flavor. Paired with crunchy broccoli and carrots, which are high in fiber, vitamins, and minerals, this dish is as nutritious as it is delicious. Plus, using an air fryer conserves the nutrients in the vegetables, making it an excellent tool for healthy cooking. Did you know? Teriyaki actually refers to the cooking technique of grilling or broiling ingredients in a glaze of soy sauce, mirin, and sugar - yummy and healthy all in one go!

Tender Lemon Herb Chicken with Sautéed Spinach and Sweet Potatoes

SERVINGS: 2 **COOKING TIME: 20 MIN** **CALORIES: 300**

Ingredients

- 2 skinless, boneless chicken breasts (1 lb or 0.5 kg)
- 2 medium sweet potatoes (1 lb or 0.5 kg)
- 4 cups of fresh Spinach (0.25 lb or 0.11 kg)
- 3 tablespoons Olive Oil (44 ml or 44 g)
- 2 tablespoons fresh Lemon Juice (1 fl oz or 30 ml)
- 2 cloves Garlic, minced (2 teaspoons or 10 g)
- 1 tablespoon fresh Rosemary, chopped
- Salt and pepper to taste

ADD TASTY BITES

WINTER SQUASHES MADE EASY:
Winter squashes like butternut or acorn can be cubed and air fried to create a quick, delicious addition to any meal. Season with a pinch of cinnamon or nutmeg to bring out their rich flavors, making them a perfect, fuss-free companion for winter roasts or as a standalone dish to ward off the cold.

Directions

1. Start by seasoning each chicken breast with salt, pepper, minced garlic, and chopped rosemary.
2. Drizzle the chicken with a tablespoon of olive oil and fresh lemon juice. Let the chicken sit for 5 minutes to let the flavors absorb.
3. While the chicken is marinating, cut the sweet potatoes into small cubes.
4. Arrange the marinated chicken in the basket of the air fryer. Slot in the sweet potatoes around the chicken.
5. Drizzle the remaining olive oil over the sweet potatoes.
6. Set your air fryer to 370°F (185°C) and cook for 15 minutes. Ensure you shake the basket halfway through for even cooking.
7. In the last 5 minutes, add the fresh spinach to the top layer of the air fryer to allow it to wilt and cook lightly.
8. Check that the chicken is cooked thoroughly and serve hot.

This dish is perfect for those looking for a healthy dinner option under 20 minutes. Packed with lean protein and fiber, it aims to keep you full while delivering nutritious benefits. The light tang of the lemon-accented chicken balances well with the caramelized sweetness of the sweet potatoes. The mild flavors and nutritional benefits of spinach adds an exciting dimension to the meal. Did you know that cooking sweet potatoes in an air fryer helps to retain their Vitamin A content better than boiling? Enjoy this quick, delicious, and nutritious meal!

Spicy Chicken Thighs with Quinoa and Honey-Glazed Carrots

SERVINGS: 2   COOKING TIME: 20 MIN   CALORIES: 430

Ingredients

Main dish

- 4 bone-in, skin-on chicken thighs
(about 1.2 pounds or 550 grams)
- 1 tablespoon smoked paprika (15 grams)
- 1 teaspoon cayenne pepper (2 grams)
- Salt and black pepper to taste

Sides

- 1 cup quinoa (170 grams)
- 1 pound carrots (450 grams), peeled and cut
into 2-inch pieces
- 1 tablespoon olive oil (15 ml)
- 2 tablespoons honey (30 ml)

ADD SAVORY SNACKLETS

FALAFEL:

Pulse drained canned chickpeas, parsley, onion, garlic,
cumin, and coriander in a food processor until combined
but still coarse. Form into small balls or patties, brush
lightly with oil, and air fry at 350°F (180°C) for about 15
minutes, turning halfway through. Serve the falafel in
pita bread with tahini sauce, tomatoes, and cucumbers
for a delicious meal.

Directions

1. Season chicken thighs evenly with smoked paprika, cayenne, salt, and black pepper.
2. Arrange chicken thighs in a single layer in the air fryer basket, skin-side up.
3. Set air fryer to 380°F or 190°C, and cook for 12 minutes.
4. Meanwhile, bring 2 cups of water to a boil in a medium saucepan. Add quinoa and a pinch of salt. Reduce heat, cover, and simmer for 15 minutes.
5. In a bowl, toss carrots with olive oil and honey. Season with salt and pepper.
6. After the chicken has been cooking for 12 minutes, carefully place the glazed carrots in the air fryer, around and between the chicken thighs. Cook for 5-8 more minutes, until the chicken is crispy and fully cooked, and the carrots are tender.
7. Fluff the quinoa with a fork and divide between two plates. Serve the chicken thighs and honey-glazed carrots alongside quinoa.

Packed with protein and rich in flavour, these spicy air-fried chicken thighs are perfect for a quick and satisfying dinner. The use of an air fryer means that you'll achieve a crispy, golden exterior without the need for deep-frying. The quinoa is a fantastic source of fibre and makes a great alternative to rice, while the honey-glazed carrots add a hint of sweetness to balance out the spices in the chicken. The best thing? This well-rounded meal supports a healthy lifestyle, as it contains just the right amount of calories, proteins, and vegetables.

Gourmet Chicken with Rosemary & Sweet Potatoes

SERVINGS: 2   COOKING TIME: 20 MIN   CALORIES: 450

Ingredients

- 2 chicken breasts (460 grams)
- 1 tbsp olive oil (15 ml)
- Salt and pepper to taste
- 2 sprigs of rosemary or 1 tsp dried (1 gram)
- 2 small sweet potatoes, cubed (300 grams)
- 1 tsp garlic powder (3 grams)
- 1 red bell pepper, sliced (150 grams)
- 1 bunch of fresh spinach (30 grams)

ADD TASTY BITES

SAVORY VEGGIE SPRING ROLLS:
Fill spring roll wrappers with a mixture of shredded cabbage, carrots, and bean sprouts. Add minced garlic, soy sauce, and a touch of sesame oil for flavor. Roll tightly and air fry at 400°F (200°C) for about 8 minutes, until the wrappers are crisp and golden. Serve with sweet chili sauce or soy sauce for dipping.

Directions

1. Begin by patting the chicken dry and spray them with a bit of olive oil. Sprinkle with salt, pepper, and garlic powder. Place the chicken in the air fryer basket.

2. Toss the sweet potato cubes in olive oil, salt, and pepper. Add the rosemary and mix until the potato cubes are well coated. Place these around the chicken in the basket.

3. Set the air fryer to 180°C or 360°F, and cook for 10 minutes.

4. Add the sliced bell pepper to the basket on top of the chicken and sweet potatoes. Continue cooking for another 5-7 minutes, or until the chicken is done and the vegetables are crispy.

5. While the dish is cooking, rinse and clean your fresh spinach. You can optionally sauté it as a side dish or use for garnish.

6. Serve the chicken and vegetables onto plates, garnish with the fresh spinach and dinner is served!

This recipe is packed with protein, fiber, and important vitamins, despite its simplicity. Chicken breasts are lean yet flavorful, particularly when seasoned and cooked in the air fryer which locks in juices and flavors. The sweet potatoes add a touch of sweetness which contrasts the savory rosemary and complements the protein, while delivering fiber and Vitamin A. Fresh spinach on top brings a touch of freshness and adds a crisp texture. Fun Fact: Did you know sweet potatoes are an excellent source of beta carotene, which converts into Vitamin A in the body? This vitamin is crucial for healthy skin, good vision, and a robust immune system. This gourmet air fryer chicken dinner is as good for your body as it is pleasing to your palate! Enjoy the richness of flavors as well as the health benefits.

Quick and Delectable Beef Stir-Fry with Veggies

SERVINGS: 2   COOKING TIME: 20 MIN   CALORIES: 290

Ingredients

Main Dish:

- 1 lb (450 g) lean beef, thinly sliced
- 2 tablespoons (30 ml) low-sodium soy sauce
- 1 tablespoon (15 ml) sesame oil
- 1 tablespoon (15 ml) cornstarch
- Pepper to taste

Side Dishes:

- 1 medium bell pepper (any color), julienned that is approximately 1/2 lb (225 g)
- 2 medium carrots, julienned which is about 1/4 lb (115 g)
- 1 medium onion, thinly sliced weighing nearly 1/2 lb (225 g)

Directions

1. In a bowl, combine the beef strips, soy sauce, sesame oil, cornstarch, and pepper. Stir until well-coated. Marinate for at least 10 minutes.
2. Arrange the marinated beef at the bottom of the air fryer basket, taking care to lay them out in a single layer.
3. Place a layer of the sliced bell pepper, carrots, and onion on an additional rack as a second layer. If there is no additional rack, place them over the beef.
4. Cook in the air fryer at 380°F (190°C) for about 10 minutes.
5. Open the fryer and stir the beef and veggies to ensure even cooking. Cook for another 5-10 minutes, or until the beef is done to your liking.
6. Serve while hot, garnish with some fresh cilantro or a squeeze of lime, if desired.

This recipe turns a simple beef stir-fry into a complete, nutritious meal by using an air fryer and adding colorful, fiber-rich vegetables. The peppers and carrots offer a sweet crunch that perfectly complements the tender, savory beef. Plus, the sesame and soy create a flavorful Asian-inspired sauce that makes this dish pop! Not only does this recipe deliver a delicious, satisfying meal in a short turnaround time, but it also promotes a healthy lifestyle with its low-calorie count and wealth of nutrients. Did you know that cooking at high heat can actually enhance some nutrients like beta carotene in carrots? So, you're not just savoring a tasty dinner, you're also boosting your health. Enjoying this quick and delectable air fryer stir-fry is a win-win situation!

Lemon Pepper Chicken with Seasoned Zucchini & Sweet Potatoes

SERVINGS: 2   COOKING TIME: 20 MIN   CALORIES: 375

Ingredients

For the Chicken:
- 2 chicken breasts (6 ounces each)
- 1 teaspoon lemon zest
- 1 tablespoon chopped fresh rosemary
- Salt and black pepper to taste

For the Zucchini and Sweet Potatoes:
- 1 medium sweet potato, cut into 1-inch pieces (1 medium or approx. 150 g)
- 1 medium zucchini, cut into 1-inch pieces (1 medium or approx. 225 g)
- 1 tablespoon olive oil
- 1 teaspoon dried oregano
- Salt and black pepper to taste

Directions

1. Lightly rub the chicken breasts with lemon zest, chopped rosemary, salt, and pepper. Set aside.
2. In a mixing bowl, combine the sweet potato and zucchini pieces, olive oil, oregano, salt, and black pepper. Toss until the vegetables are evenly coated.
3. Place the seasoned chicken breasts in the air fryer basket.
4. Carefully arrange the oiled and seasoned zucchini and sweet potatoes around the chicken, filling the empty spaces in the basket.
5. Cook at 375°F (190°C) for 15 minutes. Stir the vegetables halfway through the cooking time to ensure even cooking.
6. Check the chicken's internal temperature using a meat thermometer; it should be at least 165°F (74°C).
7. Serve the hot lemon pepper chicken with the seasoned zucchini and sweet potatoes.

This Lemon Pepper Chicken is full of flavor and so easy to prepare, making it a hit for a healthy dinner. As a protein-packed meal, chicken supports muscle growth and strength. Zucchini and sweet potatoes add a hefty dose of fiber, vitamins, and minerals to this tasty dish. The lemon and rosemary infusion in the chicken is reminiscent of Mediterranean cuisine. A worthy mention-The zest from one large lemon can pack nearly twice the aroma compared to juice from the same lemon—an interesting fact for flavor enthusiasts! Enjoy this quick, healthy dinner in under 20 minutes!

Quick Spinach-Stuffed Chicken & Sweet Potato Wedges

SERVINGS: 2   COOKING TIME: 20 MIN   CALORIES: 370

Ingredients

- 2 chicken breast fillets
  (150g / 5.2 ounces each)
- 75g / 2.6 ounces fresh baby spinach
- 28g / 1 ounce crumbled Feta cheese
- 1 tablespoon olive oil
- Salt and pepper to taste
- 2 medium sweet potatoes
  (200g / 7 ounces each)
- 1 teaspoon dried rosemary
- Fresh salad greens for serving

ADD TASTY BITES

SIZZLING SUMMER VEGGIES:
Take advantage of summer's abundance by
slicing tomatoes, bell peppers, and zucchini
for a vibrant mixed vegetable dish in the air
fryer. Just a few minutes at 400°F (200°C) will
char these slices beautifully, enhancing their
natural sweetness — ideal for a light, nutritious
side dish for those balmy evenings.

Directions

1. Butterfly the chicken breasts by cutting a slit along one side being careful not to cut all the way through.
2. Stuff each chicken breast with fresh spinach and crumbled feta.
3. Carefully close chicken breast securing with toothpicks if needed to hold it together.
4. 4. Rub the chicken breasts with olive oil, and season with salt and pepper.
5. Place chicken breasts into the basket of the air fryer.
6. Cut sweet potatoes into wedges, toss with the rosemary, salt, pepper and a little olive oil.
7. Arrange the sweet potato wedges around the chicken in the air fryer basket.
8. Cook everything in the air fryer at 180C/360F for around 15 minutes, or until chicken is cooked through and potatoes are crispy.
9. Serve hot with fresh salad greens.

This dish is not only a delicious and simple meal to prepare, but it's also very nutritious. The chicken breast provides a high-quality source of protein which is essential for muscle growth and repair. Sweet potatoes are a fantastic source of fiber and supply a steady source of energy. The spinach stuffing provides an extra boost of vitamins, and the Feta cheese adds a delightful tanginess to the dish. Did you know that the sweet potatoes can help regulate your blood sugar? This is why you feel full for longer after enjoying a dish with sweet potatoes. So, not only are you getting a quick and easy dinner, but your tummy will thank you too!

Quick Chicken Skewers with Zesty Quinoa Salad

SERVINGS: 2   COOKING TIME: 20 MIN   CALORIES: 370

Ingredients

- For Chicken Skewers:
2 boneless, skinless chicken breasts, cubed
(500g / 17.6 ounces)
1 tablespoon olive oil (15ml)
2 tablespoons soy sauce (30ml)
1 teaspoon garlic powder
1 teaspoon onion powder
Salt and black pepper to taste

- For Quinoa Salad:
1/2 cup uncooked quinoa (85g)
1 cup vegetable broth (240ml)
1 cup chopped cucumber (150g)
1 cup cherry tomatoes, halved (150g)
1/4 cup chopped red onion (approx 40g)
2 tablespoons fresh lemon juice (30ml)

Directions

1. In a bowl, coat chicken cubes with olive oil then add soy sauce, garlic powder, onion powder, salt and pepper. Toss until evenly coated.
2. Thread the chicken cubes onto skewers.
3. Arrange the skewers in a single layer inside the air fryer, making sure they aren t touching.
4. Set the air fryer to 400°F (200°C) for 10-12 minutes. While the chicken cooks, prepare the quinoa salad.
5. Rinse quinoa under cold water, then drain. Add it to a saucepan with the vegetable broth, and bring to a boil. Reduce heat to simmer, cover the pot, and let it cook for around 15 minutes.
6. In the meantime, chop cucumber, cherry tomatoes and red onion, then transfer to a bowl.
7. Once quinoa is cooked, fluff it with a fork and allow to cool slightly. Add to the vegetable mix and drizzle with fresh lemon juice. Toss to combine.
8. Divide the quinoa salad among two plates and top with cooked chicken skewers.

This recipe is perfect for fitness enthusiasts since it is high in protein, thanks to the chicken and quinoa, and low in fats. The quinoa salad offers not only nutritional benefits but also a fresh zesty flavor profile that complements the savory chicken skewers. The use of an air fryer ensures that the chicken is crisper outside and remains juicy inside, without using excessive oil. Plus, this quick feast wouldn't require you to wait by the stove, just set the air fryer and get ready to enjoy your meal! A definite crowd-pleaser recipe that even the pickiest eaters will enjoy. Happy air frying!

Chicken Fillet Julienne

SERVINGS: 2   COOKING TIME: 25 MIN   CALORIES: 400

Ingredients

- 2 chicken fillets
- 6-8 mushrooms
- Hard cheese (preferably mature) 140g
- Sour cream 100g
- Spices (musky nutmeg, dried garlic, dill, to taste)
- Salt and pepper to taste

ADD TASTY BITES

APPLE CINNAMON BITES:
Core and slice an apple, toss the slices with a bit of cinnamon and sugar, and air fry at 380°F (190°C) for 10-12 minutes. These apple bites are a healthy, quick dessert option that satisfies your sweet tooth in a wholesome way.

Directions

1. Preheat the air fryer to 180°C (350°F).
2. Clean and slice the mushrooms. Set aside.
3. Cut the chicken fillets into small pieces.
4. In a bowl, mix the chicken pieces with sliced mushrooms.
5. Add sour cream, and season with nutmeg, dried garlic, dill, salt, and pepper. Stir well to combine.
6. Divide the mixture into small, oven-safe ramekins or a baking dish suitable for an air fryer.
7. Grate the cheese and sprinkle it generously over the top of the chicken and mushroom mixture.
8. Place the ramekins or baking dish into the air fryer and cook for about 20 minutes, or until the cheese is melted and golden.
9. Check mid-way to ensure it does not overcook.

Adjust the spices according to your taste. Each spice can enhance different aspects of the flavors. The texture of the chicken and mushrooms may vary slightly in an air fryer compared to traditional baking, so monitoring during the first attempt is advised. Serve hot, ideally with a side of light salad or steamed vegetables for a balanced meal. Consider adding fresh herbs or a squeeze of lemon for an extra burst of flavor. Garnish with chopped parsley or a sprinkle of parmesan cheese before serving for a finishing touch.

Baked Chicken Liver

SERVINGS: 2   COOKING TIME: 25 MIN   CALORIES: 380

Ingredients

- Chicken liver - 400g
- 2 onions
- 2 carrots
- Cauliflower or broccoli (can substitute with zucchini, but omit the juice) - 200-300g
- 2 eggs
- Salt and spices to taste
- Olive oil for greasing

ADD TASTY BITES

PESTO STUFFED MUSHROOMS:
Remove the stems from large button mushrooms and stuff them with a mixture of cream cheese, chopped spinach, minced garlic, and grated Parmesan cheese. Air fry at 350°F (177°C) for about 8-10 minutes or until the mushrooms are tender and the filling is bubbly. These make a perfect appetizer or side dish.

Directions

1. Mince the chicken liver, onions, and carrots using a meat grinder or food processor.
2. Chop the cauliflower or broccoli into fine pieces; mix it into the liver and vegetable mixture.
3. Add two eggs, salt, and spices to the mixture and blend well.
4. Lightly grease the air fryer basket with olive oil.
5. Form the mixture into a cake or loaf shape and place it in the air fryer basket.
6. Cook in the air fryer at 180°C (356°F) for about 25 minutes or until the loaf is well cooked through. Check for doneness by inserting a knife or skewer into the center; it should come out clean.

Ensure the mixture is not too liquid; adjust the amount of cauliflower, broccoli, or zucchini to make sure it holds together well. Consider adding breadcrumbs to help hold the mixture together. Serve with fresh vegetables or a light salad for a balanced meal. Garnish with fresh herbs or a drizzle of olive oil for extra flavor. Serving the dish with a side of Greek yogurt or a light vinaigrette can add taste.

Zucchini and Chicken Casserole

SERVINGS: 2   COOKING TIME: 40 MIN   CALORIES: 350

Ingredients

- 2 medium zucchini
- Chicken breast – 400 g
- 2 medium onions
- 2 Eggs
- Greek yogurt – 3 tbsp
- Mozzarella or feta cheese – 60–80 g
- Garlic, herbs, salt, pepper – to taste
- Olive oil for greasing

ADD SAVORY SNACKLETS

SPINACH AND RICOTTA PUFFS:
Mix ricotta cheese, chopped spinach, grated Parmesan, nutmeg, salt, and pepper. Spoon the mixture into puff pastry squares, fold over to form triangles, and press the edges with a fork to seal. Brush with a bit of beaten egg for a golden finish, and air fry at 375°F (190°C) for about 15 minutes, until puffed and golden. These elegant puffs are perfect for entertaining or as a light meal.

Directions

1. Grate the zucchinis and sprinkle with a little salt, set aside to let it release its water. After 10 minutes, squeeze out the excess water.
2. Chop the onion and garlic finely.
3. Cut the chicken breast into small pieces.
4. In a bowl, combine the grated zucchini, chopped onion, chicken pieces, finely chopped garlic, and herbs.
5. Add eggs and Greek yogurt to the bowl. Mix everything thoroughly until well combined.
6. Place the mixture in the flat silicone baking mold and place into air fryer to bake.
7. Set the air fryer to 180°C and cook for 15 minutes.
8. Sprinkle the top with grated mozzarella or crumbled feta cheese, and then cook for an additional 7 minutes until the cheese is golden and bubbly.

- Squeezing the water out of the zucchini is crucial to avoid a soggy casserole.

- Adjust the seasoning according to taste before cooking, as this can't be altered once it starts cooking in the air fryer.

- Pair with a light salad to balance out the meal.

This adjusted recipe is tailored to serve two people and uses an air fryer instead of a traditional oven, offering a quicker and potentially healthier cooking method.

Honey Glazed Chicken with Garden Salad and Sweet Potato Fries

---

SERVINGS: 2   COOKING TIME: 20 MIN   CALORIES: 435

Ingredients

- 2 boneless skinless chicken breasts (approx. 500g or 18 oz.)
- 2 tablespoons honey
- 1 tablespoon lemon juice
- 1/2 teaspoon garlic powder
- 1/2 teaspoon paprika
- Salt and pepper to taste
- 2 medium sweet potatoes (approx. 300g or 10.5 oz.)
- 1 tablespoon olive oil
- Mixed salad greens, 2 cups (60g or 2 oz.)
- 1 finely sliced radish
- 1 diced cucumber
- Cherry tomatoes, halved, 1 cup (150g or 5.3 oz.)
- 1 diced avocado
- 2 tablespoons balsamic vinaigrette

Directions

1. Combine honey, lemon juice, garlic powder, paprika, salt, and pepper in a bowl and marinate the chicken breasts in it for 10 minutes.
2. While the chicken is marinating, cut the sweet potatoes into thin fries, toss them in olive oil, salt, and pepper.
3. Place the marinated chicken on the bottom of the air fryer and sweet potato fries on top.
4. Set your air fryer to 400°F (200°C) and cook everything for 15 minutes, or until chicken is fully cooked and fries are crispy.
5. Meanwhile, prepare the salad by combining the mixed greens, radish, cucumber, tomatoes, and avocado. Drizzle with the balsamic vinaigrette.
6. Once chicken and fries are done, serve them hot with the fresh garden salad.

This dish is packed with lean proteins from chicken, good carbohydrates from sweet potatoes, and fiber from the salad, making it a balanced and healthy meal. Honey gives the chicken a tantalizing sweet taste which blends perfectly with the tangy lemon, while the air fryer ensures your chicken is crispy on the outside and juicy inside. The sweet potato fries cooked in the air fryer allows lesser oil usage compared to traditional frying methods. Not to mention, a bite of the fresh salad in between gives a burst of freshness to this delicious meal. Fun Fact: Did you know honey is not only tasty but also rich in antioxidants, making it a healthy addition to your meals? Enjoy this wholesome and quick meal, high on taste and health!

Honey Citrus Glazed Chicken with Steamed Broccoli and Quinoa

SERVINGS: 2   COOKING TIME: 20 MIN   CALORIES: 450

Ingredients

For the main dish:
- 2 Chicken breasts (boneless, skinless) (approximately 500g)
- 2 tablespoons of Honey (30 ml)
- 1 tablespoon of Fresh orange juice (15ml)
- 1/2 teaspoon of Orange zest (2.5ml)
- 1/4 teaspoon of Garlic powder (1.25 ml)
- 1/4 teaspoon of Salt (1.25 ml)
- 1/4 teaspoon of Ground black pepper (1.25 ml)

For Side Dishes:
- 1 cup of Fresh broccoli florets (approximately 200g)
- 1 cup of Quinoa, cooked according to package instructions (185g)

Directions

1. Take a small bowl and stir together the honey, fresh orange juice, orange zest, garlic powder, salt, and pepper to create the glaze.
2. Generously baste the chicken breasts on all sides with the honey citrus glaze you just made.
3. Arrange the chicken breasts in the air fryer basket. Make sure they're not overlapping for even cooking.
4. Cook in the air fryer at 370°F (188°C) for 10 minutes.
5. Meanwhile, steam the broccoli either stovetop or in the microwave and cook the quinoa according to package instructions.
6. After 10 minutes, flip the chicken breasts and brush them with the remaining glaze. Continue to cook at the same temperature for another 10 minutes, or until the chicken is cooked through.
7. Once everything is ready, plate the chicken together with the steamed broccoli and quinoa.

This dish is packed with lean proteins from chicken, good carbohydrates from sweet potatoes, and fiber from the salad, making it a balanced and healthy meal. Honey gives the chicken a tantalizing sweet taste which blends perfectly with the tangy lemon, while the air fryer ensures your chicken is crispy on the outside and juicy inside. The sweet potato fries cooked in the air fryer allows lesser oil usage compared to traditional frying methods. Not to mention, a bite of the fresh salad in between gives a burst of freshness to this delicious meal. Fun Fact: Did you know honey is not only tasty but also rich in antioxidants, making it a healthy addition to your meals? Enjoy this wholesome and quick meal, high on taste and health!

Lemon Zest Chicken with Spiced Lentils and Broccoli

SERVINGS: 2   COOKING TIME: 20 MIN   CALORIES: 350

Ingredients

- 2 chicken breasts (200g each)
- 1 lemon (Zest and Juice)
- 5 sprigs of fresh thyme (roughly chopped)
- 1 tsp Black pepper (Freshly ground)
- 1 cup of dried lentils (200g)
- 2 1/2 cups of water (600ml)
- 1 tsp of cayenne pepper
- 1 head of broccoli (roughly 250g)
- 1 tbsp Olive oil (15ml)
- Salt to taste

ADD TASTY BITES

Zucchini Corn Fritters:
Combine grated zucchini (water squeezed out), corn, chopped green onions, and a binding agent like flour or chickpea flour. Season with salt, pepper, and paprika. Form into small patties and air fry at 360°F (182°C) for about 10 minutes, flipping halfway through, until they are golden and firm. Serve with a dollop of sour cream or a fresh salsa.

Directions

1. Begin by marinating your chicken breasts. In a bowl, combine lemon zest, juice, chopped thyme, black pepper, and a pinch of salt. Mix the ingredients well, then coat your chicken breasts in the mixture. Set aside for few minutes.

2. Next, prepare your lentils. In a separate bowl, combine dried lentils, water, cayenne pepper, and a pinch of salt. Mix well and set aside.

3. Now, it's time to prepare the broccoli. Cut broccoli into smaller, bite-sized florets and set aside.

4. Take your air fryer and place the marinated chicken breasts at the bottom of the basket. Above the chicken, add in your broccoli florets.

5. Cook everything in your air fryer at 360°F (180°C) for about 18 minutes. The chicken should have a nice, crisp golden brown color and the broccoli should be tender but still a little crunchy.

6. While the chicken and broccoli are cooking, transfer the lentils and their soaking water into a saucepan and bring to a boil. Lower the heat, cover, and simmer for about 15 minutes. The lentils should be tender by the end of the cooking time.

7. Take out the chicken and broccoli from the air fryer, divide evenly among two plates along with the cooked lentils.

This wholesome dish is not only full of taste but also rich in protein and fiber. The lemon zest and thyme add a wonderful citrusy and aromatic flavor to the chicken that pairs well with the spicy lentils and the wholesome broccoli. The chicken is cooked in the air fryer from the bottom, ensuring it stays juicy and tender. This quick, healthy dinner embodies fast food without the guilt, perfect for your after-work cravings! Fun fact: Did you know lentils are one of the oldest cultivated crops and were mentioned in the Bible? Now you can feel historic while enjoying your meal.

Quick Herbed Chicken with Crispy Broccoli & Carrot Coins

SERVINGS: 2   COOKING TIME: 20 MIN   CALORIES: 375

Ingredients

- 2 skinless chicken breasts (about 1/2 lb or 225 grams)
- 2 tablespoons of olive oil (30 ml)
- 1 teaspoon of dried basil (5 ml)
- 1 teaspoon of dried oregano (5 ml)
- Salt and black pepper to taste
- 2 cups of broccoli florets (around 200 grams)
- 2 large carrots, sliced into coins (around 200 grams)
- 1 tablespoon of fresh lemon juice (15 ml)
- Fresh parsley, for garnish

Add Savory Snacklets

AUTUMN ROOTS REIMAGINED:
Air fryer your way through fall with hearty root vegetables. Dice carrots, sweet potatoes, and beets, then toss them in a light drizzle of oil and your favorite herbs before air frying until they are delightfully crispy and caramelized. Serve these as a warm, comforting side or a nutritious topping for autumn salads.

Directions

1. Season the chicken breasts well with the dried herbs, salt, and pepper. Drizzle a tablespoon of olive oil over both pieces, making sure they're well coated.
2. Place the herbed chicken breasts at the bottom of your air fryer basket.
3. In a bowl, toss together the broccoli florets and carrot coins with the remaining olive oil, making sure every piece is lightly coated. Season the vegetables with a bit of salt and pepper.
4. Carefully arrange the oiled broccoli and carrot on top or around the chicken in the air fryer, leaving some room for hot air to circulate.
5. Cook at 375°F (190°C) for around 15-18 minutes or until the chicken is fully cooked and the vegetables are tender with a slightly crisp edge.
6. Once done, remove all the components and drizzle fresh lemon juice over the cooked chicken and veggies. Garnish with fresh parsley.

This quick dinner packs a punch not just in flavor but in nutritional value too. Chicken is a great source of lean protein, necessary for muscle building and repair, while broccoli and carrots supply a load of vitamins and fiber, that keeps you feeling full longer. The herbs sprinkled on the chicken do more than add taste - they offer numerous health benefits. For example, oregano is rich in antioxidants that help fend off damage from harmful free radicals in the body. Fun fact: Did you know Carrots were first grown as a medicine, not food? Yes, a carrot a day could keep you healthy and radiant! This dish is not only colorful on your plate but is also loaded with balanced nutrition that supports a healthy lifestyle, perfect for your quick dinner needs! Enjoy the herbed aroma filling your kitchen as it air fries.

Beef Fajitas with Fiber-Rich Guacamole and Zesty Lime Slaw

SERVINGS: 2　　　　**COOKING TIME: 20 MIN**　　　　**CALORIES: 500**

Ingredients

- 1 lb (450 g) of lean beef strips
- 1 tablespoon (15 ml) of olive oil
- 1 yellow bell pepper, thinly sliced
- 1 red bell pepper, thinly sliced
- 1 onion, thinly sliced
- 1 packet (about 30g) of fajita seasoning
- 4 whole grain tortillas

Side Dishes:
- 2 ripe avocados, pitted and mashed
- 1 lime, juiced
- 1/4 cup (60 ml) of chopped fresh cilantro
- Salt and pepper to taste

- 2 cups (200 g) of shredded cabbage
- 1 carrot, shredded
- 2 tablespoons (30 ml) of apple cider vinegar

Directions

1. Toss beef strips with olive oil and fajita seasoning in a bowl. Set aside to marinate briefly while you prepare the vegetables.
2. Combine sliced bell peppers and onion in the air fryer basket.
3. Place the marinated beef on top of the vegetables in the air fryer. The heat coming from the bottom will cook the beef and allow the juices to trickle down, flavoring the vegetables.
4. Set your air fryer at 400°F (200°C) and cook for 10 minutes. After 5 minutes, give the contents of the basket a quick stir for even cooking.
5. While the fajitas are cooking, prepare your side dishes. First, mix mashed avocados with lime juice, cilantro, and season with salt and pepper to taste for your guacamole. Second, toss shredded cabbage and carrot with apple cider vinegar to prepare your zesty slaw.
6. Warm tortillas in the air fryer during the last 2 minutes of cooking time.
7. Serve beef and vegetables in warmed tortillas with a side of guacamole and zesty lime slaw.

This dish is perfect for those who are looking for a quick, healthy meal that's packed with both flavor and nutritional value. Lean beef provides high-quality protein while whole grain tortillas offer a good dose of fiber. The guacamole and zesty lime slaw are not just tasty side dishes but are also great sources of vitamin C, fiber, and healthy fats. Plus, using the air fryer to cook this meal not only speeds up the process, but it also reduces the amount of oil necessary, making it a healthier choice. Fun fact - did you know that cooking in an air fryer can reduce calorie intake by up 70 to 80% compared to traditional frying methods? Now, that's something to taco 'bout!

Spicy Crispy Beef with Sweet Potato Fries and Green Salad

SERVINGS: 2   COOKING TIME: 20 MIN   CALORIES: 500

Ingredients

For the Main Dish:

- 18 oz (500 grams) of lean steak
- 1 teaspoon (5 grams) of chili powder
- 1 teaspoon (5 grams) of smoked paprika
- 1 teaspoon (5 grams) of granulated garlic
- Salt and Pepper to taste

For the Side Dishes:

- 2 large sweet potatoes, cut into long thin fries
- 2 tablespoons (30 ml) olive oil
- Salt and Pepper to taste

For the Fresh Green Salad:

- 2 cups (50 grams) of fresh mixed salad leaves
- Cherry tomatoes, halved to preference
- ½ lemon, for lemon juice
- Salt and Pepper to taste

Directions

1. Season the steak with chili powder, smoked paprika, granulated garlic, and salt and pepper on both sides.
2. Place the steak in the air fryer basket.
3. Add the sweet potato fries around the steak in the air fryer basket. Drizzle olive oil and sprinkle salt and pepper over the fries.
4. Set the air fryer to 375°F (190°C) and cook for 12 minutes.
5. After 6 minutes, flip the steak and shuffle the fries for even cooking. Continue cooking for the remaining 6 minutes.
6. While the steak and fries are air frying, prepare the salad by placing the salad leaves and cherry tomatoes in a bowl. Drizzle with lemon juice, and sprinkle with salt and pepper.
7. Once cooking is finished, let the steak rest for a few minutes before serving with the crispy sweet potato fries and refreshing salad.

This dish is a colorful and enticing ensemble that offers a balance of proteins, starch, and greens. The lean beef is a good source of iron and vitamins, and the sweet potato fries are rich in fiber and vitamins A and C. The green salad adds a fresh and crisp texture to the meal. Plus, the air fryer provides a quick and easy way to get that irresistible crispy texture without needing to deep fry! This is a dinner recipe that will make you feel good about what you're eating while also tantalizing your taste buds! Remember, eating healthy doesn't mean you have to compromise on flavor!

Beef and Veggie Medley Air Fryer Delight

SERVINGS: 2   COOKING TIME: 20 MIN   CALORIES: 300

Ingredients

- 500 grams (1.1 pounds) of lean beef, cut into strips
- 1 tablespoon of olive oil (15ml)
- Salt to taste (a pinch)
- Pepper to taste (a pinch)
- 2 medium-sized bell peppers, sliced
- 1 large carrot, sliced
- 1 medium-sized onion, diced
- 1 tablespoon of garlic, minced

Directions

1. Season the beef strips with salt and pepper.
2. Drizzle olive oil over the beef and mix until coated evenly.
3. Layer the beef strips in the air fryer and cook at 350F (180C) for 10 minutes.
4. Add bell peppers, carrot, onion, and garlic to the air fryer, placing them on top of the beef strips.
5. Cook for an additional 10 minutes at the same temperature until the vegetables are tender and the beef is cooked according to your preference.
6. Serve while hot.

This Beef and Veggie Medley Air Fryer Delight is a nutrient-packed recipe perfect for those who love protein and fiber rich meals. Lean beef provides high-quality protein and essential nutrients, while the colorful veggie medley not only makes the dish visually appealing but also adds a variety of textures and flavors to your palate. You're not just enjoying a delectable dinner; you're also taking a delicious step towards a healthier diet.

Did you know? Both bell peppers and carrots are a great source of vitamin A and C which are essential in boosting your immune system. So enjoy this vibrant meal with the delightful knowledge of its nutritional power!

Speedy Beef Stir Fry with Crispy Broccoli

SERVINGS: 2   COOKING TIME: 20 MIN   CALORIES: 320

Ingredients

- 1 pound (450 grams) of lean beef, cut into strips
- 1 tablespoon (15 ml) of olive oil
- 2 cloves of garlic, minced
- 1 inch (2.5 cm) piece of fresh ginger, grated
- 2 tablespoons (30 ml) of low-sodium soy sauce
- 1 tablespoon (15 ml) of honey
- 1 red bell pepper, cut into thin strips
- 2 cups (200 g) of fresh broccoli florets
- Salt and pepper to taste

ADD SAVORY SNACKLETS
ZUCCHINI PARMESAN CHIPS:
Slice zucchini into thin rounds, coat them lightly in olive oil, then dredge in a mixture of Parmesan cheese and breadcrumbs. Air fry at 375°F (190°C) for about 10 minutes, until crispy and golden. These make a delightful, low-carb snack that's both satisfying and nutritious.

Directions

1. Season the beef strips with salt and pepper. Set them aside.
2. In a small bowl, mix together the garlic, ginger, soy sauce, and honey.
3. Place the beef strips in the air fryer basket and brush them with the oil.
4. Set the air fryer to 350°F (175°C) and cook for 5 minutes.
5. Flip the beef strips, brush them with the soy sauce mixture, and add the red bell pepper to the basket.
6. Continue air frying for 10 minutes or until the beef is cooked to your liking.
7. Meanwhile, in a separate air fryer basket, add the broccoli florets.
8. Set the air fryer to 400°F (200°C) and cook for 5 minutes or until the florets are crispy.
9. Once everything is cooked, toss the beef, bell pepper, and broccoli together in a serving dish.
10. Serve hot, and enjoy your quick, healthy air fryer beef stir fry.

This is a simple yet flavorful dish that combines tender beef with crisp, vibrant veggies. It's not only quick to prepare but also incredibly tasty and satisfying. The lean protein from the beef helps build and maintain muscles, while the vitamins and fiber in the bell pepper and broccoli deliver a healthy punch. The subtle sweetness from the honey pairs perfectly with the salty soy sauce for a harmony of flavors that dance on your palate. Plus, air frying ensures you're getting all this deliciousness while keeping calorie count down. To make this meal suitable for a keto or low-carb diet, simply substitute the soy sauce with a sugar-free alternative like coconut aminos.

Honey Mustard Beef with Broccoli Florets and Sweet Potato

SERVINGS: 2   COOKING TIME: 20 MIN   CALORIES: 350

Ingredients

- 1 pound of lean sirloin steak (450 grams)
- 2 tablespoons of honey mustard (30 ml)
- Salt and pepper to taste
- 2 cups broccoli florets (about 200 grams)
- 1 large sweet potato, peeled and cut into wedges (about 200 grams)
- 1 tablespoon olive oil (15 ml)
- 2 cloves of garlic, minced

ADD TASTY BITES

CRISPY CHICKPEA POPPERS:
Rinse and pat dry a can of chickpeas, then toss them with olive oil, smoked paprika, and a pinch of salt. Air fry at 390°F (200°C) for about 15-20 minutes, shaking the basket halfway through. These chickpea poppers are perfect for a fiber rich, protein-packed snack on the go.

Directions

1. Season the sirloin steak with salt, pepper, and honey mustard. Let it sit for a while to marinate.
2. Meanwhile, in a bowl, toss broccoli florets and sweet potato wedges with olive oil and minced garlic to coat evenly.
3. Place the steak in the basket of the air fryer first, ensuring it lays flat.
4. Next, arrange the broccoli and sweet potato wedges evenly around the steak, fitting snugly but without overcrowding.
5. Set the air fryer to 400°F (200°C) and cook for approximately 15-18 minutes for medium doneness on the steak and until the vegetables are slightly browned and tender.
6. Check the doneness of your steak and vegetables, extending the cooking time if necessary.
7. Allow the steak to rest for a minute or two before slicing.

With its lean protein, nutrient-rich broccoli, and fiber-packed sweet potato, this dish is wholesome, balanced, and full of flavor. The honey mustard adds a tangy twist to the beef that complements the earthy vegetables perfectly. Plus, cooking it in an air fryer ensures a quick and healthy meal that's easy to make, and easier to enjoy. Did you know lean beef is not only a great source of protein but also packed with iron? So go ahead, savor every bite knowing it's not just delicious, but also nutritious! This meal could easily become a regular in your quick healthy dinner menu.

Zesty Herbed Beef Skewers with Colorful Veggie Roast

SERVINGS: 2   COOKING TIME: 20 MIN   CALORIES: 350

Ingredients

For Beef Skewers:
- 1 lb (approximately 450 grams) lean beef sirloin, cut into 1 inch cubes
- 5 cloves garlic, minced
- 2 tablespoons fresh Rosemary, finely chopped
- 2 tablespoons fresh Thyme, finely chopped
- Salt and pepper to taste

For Veggie Roast:
- 2 large bell peppers (1 red & 1 yellow), sliced into thin strips (approx. 400 grams)
- 1 medium zucchini, sliced into half moons (approx. 200 grams)
- 1 medium onion, cut into thin strips (approx. 150 grams)
- 1 tablespoon olive oil
- Salt and pepper to taste

Directions

1. In a large bowl, combine the beef cubes, minced garlic, chopped Rosemary and Thyme. Season with salt and pepper. Toss well to evenly coat the beef with the herb mixture. Set aside.

2. In another bowl, add the thinly sliced bell peppers, zucchini, and onion. Drizzle with olive oil and season with salt and pepper. Toss to ensure all veggies are well coated.

3. Thread the herbed beef cubes onto skewers. Carefully place the skewers into the air fryer basket, leaving a bit of space in between each.

4. Scatter the seasoned veggies around and between the beef skewers in the air fryer. This will allow the juices from the beef to drip onto the veggies, enhancing the flavor of the dish.

5. Set the air fryer to 375°F and cook for 15-20 minutes, or until beef is cooked to desired doneness and vegetables are tender and lightly browned.

The lean beef sirloin is a solid source of protein that will keep you feeling satiated. The brightly colored bell peppers and zucchini are not only appealing to the eye but are also packed with vitamins and fiber. This meal is truly a celebration of taste, color, and health! Enjoy it knowing that you're kitted out with beneficial nutrients, all with a texture that's a delightful surprise straight from your air fryer!

Savory Beef Tenderloin with Zesty Citrus Salad

SERVINGS: 2   **COOKING TIME: 20 MIN**   **CALORIES: 375**

Ingredients

For the beef tenderloin:

- 2 beef tenderloins
(200 g or 7 oz for Europeans)
- 1 teaspoon of olive oil (5 ml)
- Salt and pepper to taste

For the citrus salad:

- 2 cups of mixed salad greens (473 ml)
- 1 orange, segmented
- 1 small red onion, thinly sliced
- 2 tablespoons of olive oil (30 ml)
- 1 tablespoon of lemon juice (15 ml)
- Salt and pepper to taste

ADD SAVORY SNACKLETS

SAVORY VEGGIE SPRING ROLLS:
Fill spring roll wrappers with a mixture of
shredded cabbage, carrots, and bean sprouts. Add
minced garlic, soy sauce, and a touch of sesame oil
for flavor. Roll tightly and air fry at 400°F
(204°C) for about 8 minutes, until the wrappers
are crisp and golden. Serve with sweet chili sauce
or soy sauce for dipping.

Directions

1. Rub the beef tenderloins with olive oil and season with salt and pepper.

2. Place the tenderloins in the air fryer basket, allow some spaces between them for even cooking.

3. Set the air fryer to 400°F (200°C) and cook the beef for 10 minutes for medium-rare, or until desired doneness.

4. While the beef is cooking, prepare the salad by mixing the salad greens, orange segments, and red onion in a bowl.

5. In a separate bowl, whisk together the olive oil and lemon juice. Season with salt and pepper.

6. Drizzle the dressing over the salad and toss to combine.

7. Once the beef is done, let it rest for 2 to 3 minutes before slicing.

8. To serve, divide the salad between two plates, top with slices of beef.

This recipe delivers a flavorful, high-protein meal that can be prepared in less than 20 minutes. The beef tenderloin, cooked to perfection in the air fryer, pairs wonderfully with the bright, citrusy salad. Not only is this meal low-calorie, but it's also packed with vitamins from the salad. Did you know that consuming citrus fruits can help boost your immune system? So this salad is not just delicious, but also a health booster! Enjoy making this quick and easy yet impressive dinner for two. Happy Air Frying!

Spicy Asian Beef with Broccoli and Bell Peppers

SERVINGS: 2   COOKING TIME: 20 MIN   CALORIES: 380

Ingredients

- 1 lb (450g) lean beef, cut into strips
- 2 tablespoons soy sauce
- 1 tablespoon grated fresh ginger
- 1 teaspoon crushed red pepper flakes
- 1 head of broccoli, cut into florets
- 1 red bell pepper, cut into thin strips
- 2 garlic cloves, minced
- Salt and black pepper to taste
- 2 tablespoons sesame seeds
- 1 tablespoon olive oil

ADD SAVORY SNACKLETS

CRISPY TOFU NUGGETS:
Press and cube firm tofu, then toss the pieces in soy sauce. Coat them in a mix of panko breadcrumbs, nutritional yeast, and garlic powder. Air fry at 400°F (204°C) for 12–15 minutes, shaking halfway through until they're crispy and golden. Serve these nuggets with a spicy dipping sauce or over a bed of steamed rice and veggies.

Directions

1. In a bowl, combine the beef strips, soy sauce, ginger, pepper flakes, garlic, salt, and black pepper. Mix to coat the beef evenly and set aside to marinate for 10 minutes.

2. Meanwhile, toss the broccoli and bell pepper in olive oil and a pinch of salt.

3. Add the beef strips to the air fryer, spreading them in an even layer at the bottom.

4. Place the broccoli and bell pepper on top, again in an even layer.

5. Set the air fryer to 360°F (180°C) and cook for 10 minutes.

6. Shake the basket and cook for an additional 5 minutes, or until the beef is browned and the vegetables are tender.

7. Sprinkle the dish with sesame seeds before serving.

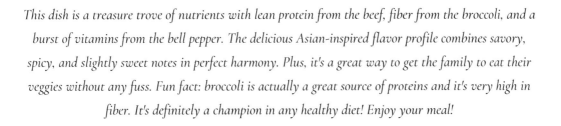

This dish is a treasure trove of nutrients with lean protein from the beef, fiber from the broccoli, and a burst of vitamins from the bell pepper. The delicious Asian-inspired flavor profile combines savory, spicy, and slightly sweet notes in perfect harmony. Plus, it's a great way to get the family to eat their veggies without any fuss. Fun fact: broccoli is actually a great source of proteins and it's very high in fiber. It's definitely a champion in any healthy diet! Enjoy your meal!

Air Fryer Zesty Italian Herb Beef and Veggie Dinner

SERVINGS: 2   COOKING TIME: 20 MIN   CALORIES: 350

Ingredients

- 1 pound (450 grams) of lean beef sirloin, cut into strips
- 1 tablespoon (14.8 ml) of olive oil
- 1 teaspoon (4.20 grams) of Italian herb seasoning
- Salt and pepper to taste
- 1 large bell pepper (170 grams), sliced
- 1 medium red onion (150 grams), sliced
- 2 medium zucchinis (400 grams), sliced
- 8 small new potatoes (800 grams), halved
- 1 garlic clove (3 grams), minced

ADD SAVORY SNACKLETS

PARMESAN GARLIC ASPARAGUS:
Toss asparagus spears with olive oil, minced garlic, grated Parmesan, and a pinch of salt. Air fry at 400°F (204°C) for 7–8 minutes until the asparagus is tender and the Parmesan is crispy. Serve immediately for a delicious and healthy side dish.

Directions

1. Toss the beef strips with olive oil, Italian herb seasoning, minced garlic, and a sprinkle of salt and pepper in a large bowl.

2. Place the seasoned beef at the bottom of your air fryer basket.

3. Above the beef, arrange a layer of the bell pepper and onion slices.

4. Top the layers with zucchini slices and halved new potatoes.

5. Set your air fryer to 400°F (200°C), and cook for 15 minutes, shaking the basket a few times for even cooking.

6. Check the doneness of meat and vegetables, cook for another 2–3 minutes if needed.

7. Serve warm and enjoy your quick and healthy dinner!

This is an appealing, wholesome meal, bursting with colors and flavors. Filled with a well-balanced mix of protein from lean beef and fiber from fresh vegetables, it is highly reminiscent of Italian countryside cuisine. The convenience of the air fryer locks in the tenderness of the sirloin and crisps up the veggie edges for texture variety. A fun fact - did you know that zucchini is extremely low in calories but high in fiber, making it a great choice for weight control? Now you're just 20 minutes away from a hearty and healthy dinner!

Tangy Moroccan-Spiced Beef Stir Fry

SERVINGS: 2   COOKING TIME: 20 MIN   CALORIES: 350

Ingredients

- 1 pound of lean beef strips (500 grams)
- 1 yellow bell pepper, thinly sliced
- 1 red onion, chopped into thin wedges
- 2 tablespoons of olive oil (30 ml)
- Salt and pepper to taste
- 1 tablespoon of Moroccan spice mix (15 ml)
- 2 cloves of garlic, minced
- Roasted vegetables for a side dish:
  - 10 baby carrots (250 grams)
  - 10 Brussels sprouts (250 grams)
  - 1 tablespoon of olive oil (15 ml)
- Fresh cilantro leaves for garnish

ADD TASTY BITES

MINI CHICKEN QUESADILLAS:
Take small flour tortillas and fill them with a mixture of cooked, shredded chicken, grated cheese, and a spoonful of salsa. Fold the tortillas in half to make half-moons and secure them with a toothpick. Air fry at 360°F (180°C) for about 4-6 minutes or until the tortillas are golden and the cheese has melted. These mini quesadillas are perfect for a quick snack or appetizer.

Directions

1. Toss together the beef strips, bell pepper, red onion, olive oil, salt, pepper, Moroccan spice mix, and minced garlic in a mixing bowl.

2. Add the vegetables to the air fryer basket, making sure they have space around them for even cooking.

3. Add the beef mixture to the air fryer, positioning it above the basket in the fryer to ensure it cooks from the bottom up.

4. Set the air fryer to 400 F (200 C) for 8 minutes, then stir the ingredients to help them cook evenly.

5. Continue cooking for another 7 minutes, or until the beef is fully cooked and the vegetables are tender.

6. Garnish with fresh cilantro before serving.

With a full serving of protein-packed beef and fiber-rich vegetables, this Tangy Moroccan-Spiced Beef Stir Fry offers a massive punch of goodness in a small amount of time. The Moroccan spices add an exotic touch to the dish, making weeknight dinners seem like a culinary vacation, while also providing metabolism-boosting benefits. As you savor the dish's juicy, guilt-free taste, your mind may wander to the outdoor markets and music-filled streets of Morocco, where this flavorful spice blend originates.

Spiced Beef Tenderloin with Sweet Potato Fries and Garlic Spinach

SERVINGS: 2   COOKING TIME: 20 MIN   CALORIES: 550

Ingredients

Beef Tenderloin:
- 400 g / 14 oz Beef Tenderloin
- 1 tbsp Olive Oil
- Salt to taste
- 1/2 teaspoon Black Pepper
- 1/2 tbsp Garlic Powder
- 1/2 tbsp Onion Powder

Sweet Potato Fries:
- 2 Sweet Potatoes
- 1 tbsp Olive Oil
- Salt to taste
- 1 tsp Paprika

Garlic Spinach:
- 1 bag of fresh Spinach (approximately 200g / 7 oz)
- 2 cloves Garlic
- 1 tbsp Olive Oil

Directions

1. Rub the beef tenderloin with olive oil, salt, pepper, garlic powder, and onion powder, ensuring it is evenly coated.

2. Place the beef in the air fryer basket.

3. Peel and cut the sweet potatoes into fries. Toss them in olive oil, salt, and paprika.

4. Arrange the sweet potatoes around the beef in the air fryer.

5. Cook everything in the air fryer at 180°C / 360°F for 10 minutes.

6. While the beef and sweet potatoes are cooking, heat the olive oil in a pan over medium heat. Add the garlic and sauté until fragrant.

7. Add the spinach to the pan and stir until wilted—it should only take 3-5 minutes.

8. Check the beef for desired doneness after 10 minutes, flipping it and the sweet potatoes for an even cook.

9. Continue to cook everything in the air fryer for another 8-10 minutes.

10. Serve the beef tenderloin with the sweet potato fries on the side and garlic spinach on top of the beef.

This recipe is a hearty and healthful meal that's ready in just 20 minutes. The beef provides high-quality protein, while the sweet potatoes and spinach contribute valuable fiber, vitamin A, and iron. Balanced in nutrition and rich in flavor, this is a perfect healthy dinner for two. Plus, the versatility of air fryers means less oil and mess, so you can enjoy this delicious meal without worrying about the clean-up afterward. A little tip, serve with a squeeze of lemon juice or a dollop of Greek yogurt on the side for an added zesty flavor. Bon Appétit!

Succulent Beef Sirloin with Crispy Broccoli & Golden Sweet Potatoes

SERVINGS: 2   COOKING TIME: 20 MIN   CALORIES: 450

Ingredients

Main Dish:

- 16 oz (454g) beef sirloin, cut into 2 inch pieces
- 1/2 teaspoon salt
- 1/2 teaspoon ground pepper
- 1 tablespoon garlic powder
- 1 tablespoon onion powder

Side Dishes:

- 1 large head of broccoli, cut into florets
- 2 medium sweet potatoes, peeled and diced
- 1 tablespoon olive oil
- 1/2 teaspoon (2.5g) paprika
- 1/2 teaspoon (2.5g) salt

ADD TASTY BITES

CAULIFLOWER BUFFALO WINGS:
Cut a head of cauliflower into bite-sized florets. Dip each floret into a batter made from flour, water, garlic powder, and paprika. Air fry at 360°F (182°C) for about 20 minutes, flipping halfway through. Toss the crispy florets in buffalo sauce and serve with vegan ranch dressing for a spicy, crowd-pleasing snack.

Directions

1. Season the beef sirloin pieces with salt, pepper, garlic powder, and onion powder, ensuring each piece is well coated.

2. Place the seasoned beef in the air fryer basket.

3. In a mixing bowl, combine broccoli florets and diced sweet potatoes. Drizzle with olive oil and sprinkle salt and paprika, tossing gently to evenly coat.

4. Surround the beef with the broccoli and sweet potatoes in the air fryer basket, ensuring that they are not stacked on top of each piece.

5. Cook everything in the air fryer at 375°F (190°C) for 15 minutes, then increase the temperature to 400°F (200°C) for the final 5 minutes to crisp up the vegetables.

6. Once cooking is complete, let it rest for 2 to 3 minutes before serving.

This dish is a low-carb, high-protein, and nutrient-dense meal that helps support a healthy lifestyle. Did you know that broccoli is a powerhouse of fibers, vitamins, and antioxidants? Plus, the sweet potato is packed with vitamin A and fiber, aiding in digestion and supporting eye health. Recommended pairing: a glass of bold Cabernet Sauvignon that nicely complements the rich flavors and textures of this meal! Enjoy every flavorful bite!

Quick and Easy Air Fryer Beef Stir Fry

SERVINGS: 2   COOKING TIME: 20 MIN   CALORIES: 250

Ingredients

- 1 lb (about 453 grams) of lean beef steak, sliced into thin strips
- 1 medium onion, sliced (150 grams)
- 2 bell peppers, assorted colors, cut in thin strips
- 2 tablespoons of vegetable oil (30 ml)
- Salt and pepper to taste

- 3 tablespoons of low-sodium soy sauce (45 ml)
- 1 tablespoon of honey (15 ml)
- 1 tablespoon of fresh ginger, grated
- 2 cloves of garlic, minced

ADD TASTY BITES

MINI SKEWERS ON TOOTHPICKS:
Marinate small cubes of chicken or beef along with bell pepper, onion, and cherry tomatoes in a blend of olive oil, soy sauce, honey, garlic, paprika, salt, and pepper. Thread the marinated ingredients onto toothpicks and air fry at 400°F for about 8-10 minutes until the meat is cooked and the vegetables are tender. These tasty bites offer a burst of flavor in each mouthful and make for a fun, easy-to-eat treat that's sure to impress your guests.

Directions

1. Start by placing the sliced beef strips into the air fryer basket. Toss them with the vegetable oil, salt, and pepper.

2. Set your air fryer to 400°F (200°C), and cook the beef for 7 minutes, shaking the basket after 3 minutes to ensure even cooking.

3. In the meantime, prepare the sauce by mixing together the soy sauce, honey, grated ginger, and minced garlic. Set it aside for later.

4. Once the beef is cooked, add in the sliced peppers and onions. Toss them around to evenly distribute, set the air fryer to the same temperature, and cook for an additional 7 minutes.

5. After, pour the prepared sauce over the cooked beef and veggies in the air fryer basket. Toss all ingredients to evenly coat and cook on the same setting for 3 additional minutes.

6. Once it's ready, serve immediately for best taste.

The natural sweetness from the honey, combined with the saltiness of the soy sauce, imparts a delectable savory-sweet flavor to the stir fry. The pops of colored bell peppers not only make this meal visually appealing, but also add a lovely crunch. Remember, cooking should not only be about maintaining a healthy lifestyle, but also enjoying the process, the flavors, and most importantly, the final result! So relish this stress-free, guilt-free, 20-minute dinner today!

Zesty Lemon-Garlic Turkey Tenders with Root Vegetable Fries

SERVINGS: 2   COOKING TIME: 20 MIN   CALORIES: 360

Ingredients

For the Turkey Tenders:
- 1 pound (450 grams) of turkey tenders
- Zest and juice of 1 large lemon
- 2 cloves of garlic, finely minced
- 2 tablespoons (30 ml) of olive oil
- A pinch of salt and fresh ground black pepper

For the Root Vegetable Fries:
- 1 medium sweet potato
- 2 large parsnips (around 200 grams)
- 1 tablespoon (15 ml) of vegetable oil
- Salt and pepper to taste

ADD TASTY BITES

MINI CAPRESE SKEWERS:
Thread a cherry tomato, a small ball of mozzarella, and a fresh basil leaf onto small skewers. Drizzle with balsamic glaze and a touch of olive oil. Air fry at 360°F (182°C) for just 2-3 minutes to warm through without melting the cheese completely. This quick dish offers a burst of fresh flavors

Directions

1. In a bowl, place the turkey tenders and top with lemon zest and juice, minced garlic, olive oil, salt, and pepper. Ensure all turkey pieces are evenly coated. Marinate for at least 5 minutes.

2. While the turkey is marinating, peel and cut the sweet potato and parsnips into equal-sized thin sticks. Toss them in the vegetable oil, salt, and pepper. Arrange them in the air fryer basket, ensuring they are spread out with space in between each piece.

3. Place marinated turkey tenders on top of the root vegetables, ensuring the turkey pieces are not overlapping.

4. Cook everything in the air fryer at 400°F (200°C) for about 10 minutes. Then give everything a good stir and cook for another 5-7 minutes, until turkey is fully cooked and vegetables are crispy.

This recipe offers a hearty, protein-rich and low-fat dinner that's ready in just 20 minutes. Turkey is an excellent lean protein source, while sweet potatoes and parsnips offer dietary fiber and essential nutrients. The lemon-garlic marinade lends itself to a light and zesty flavor profile, enhancing the natural taste of the turkey. Remember, good food doesn't need to be complicated, and this recipe is a prime example of fast and healthy comfort food. Enjoy!

Crispy Chicken Parmesan With Fresh Tomato Roasted Green Beans

SERVINGS: 2   COOKING TIME: 20 MIN   CALORIES: 530

Ingredients

Main Dish:

- 2 boneless skinless chicken breasts (450 grams)
- 1/2 cup whole wheat flour (120 grams)
- 2 large eggs
- 1 cup panko breadcrumbs (240 grams)
- 1/4 cup grated Parmesan cheese (60 grams)
- Salt and pepper to taste
- 1/2 cup marinara sauce (120 grams)
- 1/2 cup shredded mozzarella cheese (120 grams)

Side Dish:

- 1/2 pound fresh green beans (225 grams)
- 1 pint cherry tomatoes (475 grams)
- 2 tablespoons olive oil (30 ml)
- Salt and pepper to taste
- 1 tablespoon minced garlic (15 grams)

ADD TASTY BITES

BUFFALO CHICKEN BITES:
Toss bite-sized pieces of chicken breast in flour, then dip in beaten eggs and coat with breadcrumbs. Air fry at 360°F (182°C) for about 10 minutes, then toss with buffalo sauce and return to the air fryer for another 2-3 minutes. Serve with celery sticks and blue cheese dressing for a game-day favorite.

Directions

1. Start by coating the chicken breasts in flour, shaking off any excess. Dip in beaten eggs, then cover in a mixture of panko breadcrumbs and Parmesan. Season with salt and pepper.

2. Arrange the coated chicken breasts in the air fryer, ensuring there's enough room around each piece for air to circulate.

3. Cook at 375°F (190°C) for 10 minutes, or until the chicken is golden brown and almost cooked through.

4. While the chicken is cooking, toss the green beans and cherry tomatoes in olive oil, garlic, salt, and pepper.

5. Once the chicken is almost done, pause the air fryer to safely spread the marinara sauce over each chicken breast, followed by a generous sprinkling of mozzarella.

6. Carefully lay the prepared green beans and cherry tomatoes around the chicken in the fryer.

7. Continue air frying for another 10 minutes, until the cheese on the chicken is melted and bubbly, and the vegetables are tender and slightly charred.

No need to fire up the oven - this dish is a perfect example of how an air fryer can effortlessly deliver a melt-in-the-mouth Chicken Parmesan, complete with a side of delicious roasted veggies. This recipe leans toward healthier choices, using whole wheat flour and panko breadcrumbs for the chicken coating. The freshness of the cherry tomatoes provides a burst of flavour that pairs well with the crisp green beans, adding not just taste but also important fibers and vitamins. Cooking with an air fryer reduces the overall cooking time, ensuring dinner can be prepared and enjoyed in a flash. Now, isn't that a fun, quick way to whip up a culinary masterpiece?

Herb-Crusted Turkey Tenders and Roasted Veg with a Fresh Salad

SERVINGS: 2   COOKING TIME: 20 MIN   CALORIES: 320

Ingredients

- 2 turkey breast tenders (500 grams)
- 1 teaspoon dried oregano (5 mL)
- 1 teaspoon dried basil (5 mL)
- 1 tablespoon olive oil (15 mL)
- Salt and pepper to taste
- Broccoli and carrots for roasting, chopped (3 cups broccoli, 2 cups carrots)
- Mixed greens for salad (2 cups)
- Cherry tomatoes for salad (1 cup)
- 1 fresh lemon, juiced
- Optional: Sesame seeds for salad topping

ADD TASTY BITES

FIG AND GOAT CHEESE BRUSCHETTA: Slice fresh figs and air fry at 360°F (182°C) for about 4-5 minutes to intensify their sweetness. Spread goat cheese on toasted baguette slices, top with warm figs, a drizzle of honey, and a sprinkle of crushed walnuts for a sweet and savory treat.

Directions

1. Begin by tossing the turkey tenders with olive oil, dried oregano, dried basil, and season with salt and pepper.
2. Place the turkey tenders in the air fryer.
3. Surround them with your chopped broccoli and carrots.
4. Set the air fryer to 375°F (190°C) for 15 minutes.
5. While that's cooking, prepare a fresh side salad by tossing mixed greens, cherry tomatoes, lemon juice for dressing, and top with sesame seeds.
6. After 15 minutes, check the turkey tenders and vegetables. They should be beautifully browned and tender. If not, set the air fryer for another 5 minutes.
7. Serve the turkey tenders and roasted vegetables straight from the air fryer with the fresh side salad.

This Herb-Crusted Turkey Tenders and Roasted Veg with a Fresh Salad encompass a complete, balanced meal in no time at all! Turkey is an excellent source of lean protein that helps keep you full. Roasting the veggies in an air fryer gives them a delightful crispiness while preserving their nutrients. The side salad brings in necessary fibers, antioxidants, and enzymes for a healthier meal. Lastly, no need to worry about using too much oil as the air fryer needs very minimal amount of it! Did you know that using dried herbs can actually have a more concentrated flavor, which is perfect for the quick cooking time of the air fryer? Enjoy this quick, healthy dinner when you're crunched for time but still wanting a satisfying, balanced meal.

Crispy Air Fryer Rabbit with Steamed Mixed Veggies

| SERVINGS: 2 | COOKING TIME: 20 MIN | CALORIES: 520 |

Ingredients

Main Dish:
- 1 rabbit (2lbs / 1kg), cut into pieces
- 1 tablespoon of olive oil (15ml)
- 1 teaspoon of smoked paprika (5ml)
- Salt and black pepper to taste

Side Dish:
- 2 cups of mixed frozen vegetables (broccoli, carrots, peas) (480ml)
- 1 teaspoon of garlic powder (5ml)

ADD TASTY BITES

BALSAMIC GLAZED CAPRESE BRUSCHETTA: Top toasted baguette slices with slices of fresh mozzarella and tomato. Air fry at 360°F (182°C) for about 3-4 minutes until the cheese begins to melt. Top with fresh basil leaves and a drizzle of balsamic glaze for a classic Caprese experience.

Directions

1. Start by seasoning your rabbit pieces with smoked paprika, salt, and black pepper. Ensure all the pieces are well coated.

2. Drizzle the seasoned rabbit with olive oil and ensure it's evenly distributed.

3. Arrange the rabbit pieces in the air fryer, positioned for optimal hot air circulation.

4. Set your air fryer to 200°C (392°F), and cook the rabbit for 5 minutes.

5. While the rabbit is cooking, season your frozen mixed vegetables with garlic powder. Wrap the vegetables in aluminum foil and place them on an additional rack if available, or on top of the meat. If you want the vegetables to be crispy, do not use foil.

6. After 5 minutes, add the mixed vegetables on top of the rabbit in the air fryer.

7. Cook for another 15 minutes until both the rabbit and the vegetables are cooked through.

This crispy air fryer rabbit paired with steamed mixed veggies is not just quick and easy, but also full of nutritious values. High in protein and low in fat, rabbit meat is a healthy choice that provides a good source of Iron and Vitamin B3. Mixed veggies are also rich in vitamins and fiber, contributing to a balanced and healthy meal. A little tip for a juicy rabbit: don't overcook it, as it might become dry. Enjoy this crispy, flavourful dish, and don't forget to share, as this recipe is perfect for two!

Juicy Turkey Tenderloin with Garlic & Herb Roasted Carrots

SERVINGS: 2   COOKING TIME: 20 MIN   CALORIES: 320

Ingredients

- 1 turkey tenderloin
(about 8 ounces/227 grams)
- 1 teaspoon olive oil (5 ml)
- Salt and pepper to taste
- 2 teaspoons of mixed dried herbs, such as
thyme and rosemary
- 2 large carrots (200 grams),
sliced into thin sticks
- 2 cloves of garlic (6 grams), minced
- A handful of fresh parsley (15 grams), finely
chopped
- Fresh lemon wedges for serving

ADD TASTY BITES

BUFFALO CHICKEN BITES:
Toss bite-sized pieces of chicken breast in flour,
then dip in beaten eggs and coat with
breadcrumbs. Air fry at 360°F (182°C) for about 10
minutes, then toss with buffalo sauce and return
to the air fryer for another 2-3 minutes. Serve
with celery sticks and blue cheese dressing for a
game-day favorite.

Directions

1. Lightly coat the turkey tenderloin with olive oil and season with salt, pepper, and half of the dried herbs. Set aside.

2. In a bowl, combine the sliced carrots, minced garlic, remaining dried herbs, and a little salt and pepper. Toss them together until the carrots are well-coated.

3. Arrange the garlic and herb tossed carrots in the bottom of the air fryer's basket, spreading them out in an even layer.

4. Place the seasoned turkey tenderloin on top of the layered carrots.

5. Cook at 400°F (200°C) for approximately 10-12 minutes, then flip the turkey and cook for another 5-7 minutes.

6. When the cooking is completed, carefully remove the turkey and let it rest for a few minutes before slicing. Give the carrots a good stir and serve them alongside the turkey slices, garnishing with the fresh parsley. Offer fresh lemon wedges for squeezing over the top.

This recipe offers a perfect balance of lean protein from the turkey tenderloin and fiber-rich vegetables. The garlic and herb roasted carrots provide a delightful mix of zesty and aromatic flavors. The cooking method in the air fryer ensures the turkey is juicy, while providing a slight crisp to the carrots. The parsley brings a freshness to the dish and the squeeze of lemon at the end lifts the flavors beautifully! Did you know, carrots are a great source of vitamin A, which supports eye health? Enjoy this 20-minute dinner that not only tantalizes the taste buds but also contributes to a healthy diet! This dish pairs well with a glass of white wine. Bon Appétit!

Quick and Savory Air-Fried Turkey Breast and Mixed Vegetables

SERVINGS: 2   COOKING TIME: 20 MIN   CALORIES: 420

Ingredients

- For the Turkey Breast:
1 turkey breast filet (about 1 lb or 450g)
2 cloves garlic, finely chopped
(2 teaspoons or 10g)
1 tablespoon olive oil
(1 tablespoon or 15 ml)
Salt and pepper to taste

- For the Mixed Vegetables:
1 cup broccoli florets (1 cup or 150g)
1 cup carrot slices (1 cup or 130g)
1 red bell pepper, chopped (1 cup or 150g)
1 tablespoon olive oil
(1 tablespoon or 15 ml)
Salt and pepper to taste

Directions

1. Lightly season the turkey breast filet with the garlic, salt, pepper, and 1 tablespoon of olive oil. Set aside to marinate for a few minutes while you prep the vegetables.

2. In a separate bowl, mix the broccoli florets, carrot slices, and chopped red bell pepper. Drizzle with 1 tablespoon of olive oil, and season with salt and pepper. Stir to coat the vegetables evenly.

3. Place the turkey breast filet at the bottom of the air fryer basket, then scatter the mixed vegetables around and on top.

4. Set the air fryer to 375°F (190°C) and cook for 20 minutes, or until the turkey is cooked through and the vegetables are tender and slightly crisp.

This quick and easy dinner recipe is not just convenient but also packs a nutritional punch. Turkey is a great source of lean protein, while the mixed vegetables provide fibre, antioxidants and a variety of vitamins. Oven-free cooking using an air fryer helps preserve these nutrients, while also achieving a delicious, roasted flavor in less time. Perfect for days where you need a healthy meal but are short on time, this air-friend turkey and veggies combo is sure to be a family favorite. Be sure to keep watch during the final minutes of cooking to ensure your vegetables don't over-crisp!

Tangy Turkey Cutlets and Vibrant Veggie Medley

SERVINGS: 2   COOKING TIME: 20 MIN   CALORIES: 320

Ingredients

For the Tangy Turkey Cutlets:

1 lb (450g) Turkey Breast Cutlets

1 tsp (5g) Ground Paprika

1 tsp (5g) Onion Powder

1 tbsp (15ml) Olive Oil

Salt and Pepper to taste

For the Vibrant Veggie Medley:

2 large Carrots, sliced into thin rounds
(1 cup/128g)

1 medium Zucchini, cut into half moons
(1 cup/113g)

1 small Red Bell Pepper, cut into thin strips
(1 cup/149g)

1 tbsp (15ml) Olive Oil

1 tbsp (15ml) Lemon Juice

Fresh Chopped Parsley for garnishing (optional)

Directions

1. Marinate Turkey breast cutlets in a mixture of ground paprika, onion powder, olive oil, salt, and pepper. Set aside for 5 minutes to absorb the flavors.

2. Arrange the Turkey cutlets in a single layer at the bottom of the air fryer basket.

3. In a bowl, toss the sliced Carrots, Zucchini, and Red Bell Pepper with olive oil and lemon juice.

4. Layer the Veggie Medley over the Turkey Cutlets in the Air Fryer.

5. Cook for 10 minutes at 360°F (180°C). Then, gently flip the cutlets and toss the vegetables. Cook for another 10 minutes or until the turkey is adequately cooked and the vegetables are tender-crisp. A layering method helps the turkey to remain juicy and tender by being steamed by the vegetables.

6. Garnish with fresh chopped parsley before serving, if desired.

This Tangy Turkey Cutlets and Vibrant Veggie Medley Dish will impress your palate with the flavorful juxtaposition between savory turkey and tangy, fresh vegetables, not to mention its high nutritional value. The protein-packed turkey and fiber-rich vegetable medley is a guilt-free comfort food for all health-conscious foodies out there. Keep in mind that turkey is a lean source of protein and when paired with a plethora of colorful veggies, it presents a balanced meal. This recipe proves that quick and healthy can certainly be synonymous with delicious. And remember, cooking should be fun- don't be afraid to play with your food! Enjoy the process and the results.

Homestyle Chicken and Vegetable Casserole

SERVINGS: 2   COOKING TIME: 20 MIN   CALORIES: 390

Ingredients

- Chicken Breast, 2 pieces
(500 grams/1.1 pounds)
- Italian seasoning, 2 teaspoons (10ml)
- Olive oil, 1 tablespoon (15ml)
- Salt and pepper to taste
- Red bell pepper, 1 medium-sized
(150 grams/5.29 ounces)
- Broccoli, 1 head
(180 grams/6.35 ounces)
- Sweet corn, 1 small can
(198 grams/7 ounces, drained)
- Grated cheddar cheese, 1 cup
(110 grams/4 ounces)

ADD TASTY BITES

BACON-WRAPPED STUFFED JALAPEÑOS:
Stuff halved jalapeños with a mixture of cream
cheese and shredded cheddar, then wrap each
with half a slice of bacon. Secure with a toothpick
and air fry at 375°F (190°C) for about 10-12
minutes, or until the bacon is crispy. This spicy,
creamy snack is perfect for entertaining or
enjoying on a relaxing evening.

Directions

1. Start by cutting the chicken breasts into small bite-sized pieces, then season with Italian seasoning, salt, pepper, and olive oil.

2. Place the seasoned chicken pieces at the bottom of the air fryer basket.

3. Cut the broccoli into small florets and the red bell pepper into small chunks. Combine these with the drained sweet corn.

4. Layer the vegetables over the chicken pieces in the air fryer basket.

5. Sprinkle the grated cheddar cheese over the top of the vegetables.

6. Set the air fryer to 375°F (190°C) and cook for 20 minutes. Check the chicken is fully cooked before serving.

This Homestyle Chicken and Vegetable Casserole is a wholesome, comfort-food dinner that can be whipped up in no time. It offers a balance of hearty protein from the chicken, fiber from the vibrant veggies, and calcium from the cheese. This dish is not just healthy but is also colorful and full of nutrients. As the food in air fryers is cooked by circulating hot air, it uses less oil, making meals healthier. The Italian seasoning provides a dash of herbs and spices that gives a zesty flavor to the dish. Finally, the melted cheddar cheese adds a creamy texture that brings all the ingredients together, making it a crowd-pleaser! So, when you want a fulfilling and nutritious dinner for two in just 20 minutes, remember this recipe. Enjoy!

Healthy Fish and Vegie
Dinner Recipes

Zesty Lemon Garlic Salmon with Quinoa Salad

SERVINGS: 2   COOKING TIME: 20 MIN   CALORIES: 535

Ingredients

Main Dish:

- 2 salmon fillets (6 ounces each - 170 grams each)
- 1 garlic clove, minced (3 grams)
- Zest and juice of 1 lemon (50 grams)
- Salt and black pepper to taste
- Extra virgin olive oil spray

Side Dish:

- 1 cup Quinoa, rinsed (185 grams)
- 2 cups water (473 ml)
- 1 medium cucumber, diced (150 grams)
- 1 cup cherry tomatoes, halved (150 grams)
- 2 tablespoons olive oil (30 ml)
- Juice of 1/2 lemon (25 ml)
- Salt and black pepper to taste

Directions

1. Preheat your air fryer to 360°F or 180°C.
2. Rinse two salmon fillets and pat dry. Season with minced garlic, lemon zest, lemon juice, salt, and pepper. Spray with a light coating of olive oil.
3. Place the salmon fillets in the air fryer basket. Cook for 10 minutes or until the salmon is cooked to your desired level.
4. Meanwhile, place water and quinoa in a saucepan and bring to a rapid simmer. Once simmering, reduce heat and cook until quinoa is tender, about 12 minutes.
5. Drain quinoa well and let cool. In a large bowl, combine quinoa with diced cucumber, halved cherry tomatoes, olive oil, lemon juice, salt, and pepper. Stir until well combined.
6. Once salmon is ready, serve with quinoa salad on the side.

This zesty lemon garlic salmon is packed with healthy Omega-3 fatty acids which contribute to heart health. Combined with high fiber, protein-rich quinoa salad, it becomes an excellent balanced meal delivering a satisfying blend of flavors and textures. Cooking in an air fryer also reduces the need for excessive oil, ensuring a healthier meal. A fun fact to note: Did you know salmon gets its pink color from a diet rich in shellfish? Now you can impress your dinner guest with this trivia along with a flavorful meal. Enjoy!

Garlic Butter Shrimp with Zucchini Noodles

SERVINGS: 2   COOKING TIME: 20 MIN   CALORIES: 350

Ingredients

- 1 pound (450g) of large Shrimp, peeled and deveined
- 2-3 Zucchinis, spiralized into noodles (2lb/900g)
- 4 cloves of Garlic, minced (3.5g)
- 2 tablespoons of Olive Oil (30ml)
- 1/2 cup of unsalted Butter (115g)
- 1 teaspoon of Red Pepper Flakes (5g), optional
- Salt and Ground Pepper, to taste
- Fresh Parsley Leaves, for garnish
- Fresh Lemon Wedges, for serving

ADD TASTY BITES

CLASSIC TOMATO BRUSCHETTA:
Slice a baguette into rounds, brush with olive oil, and air fry at 360°F (182°C) for about 3-4 minutes until lightly toasted. Top with a mixture of chopped tomatoes, fresh basil, minced garlic, olive oil, salt, and balsamic vinegar. Return to the air fryer for another 2-3 minutes to warm through.

Directions

1. In a small bowl, toss the shrimp with minced garlic, salt, and pepper. Set it aside.
2. Melt butter in a large skillet over medium heat. Add olive oil and red pepper flakes, and stir well.
3. Put shrimp into the flat silicone baking mold and brush them with the garlic butter.
4. Spread the zucchini noodles over the shrimp. Cook at 400°F (200°C) for 6-9 minutes, until the shrimp are pink and cooked through.
5. Carefully remove the shrimp and zucchini from the air fryer, stirring them to ensure the noodles are well coated in the garlic butter.
6. Serve the shrimp and zucchini noodles hot, garnished with fresh parsley and a squeeze of lemon.

This Garlic Butter Shrimp with Zucchini Noodles dish is a marvelous blend of rich, buttery garlic flavors and fresh, vibrant zucchini. The shrimp provide a high-quality source of protein, while the zucchini adds a wonderful pop of color and is packed with fiber. This is a low-carb meal, perfect for those following a keto diet or simply aiming to eat healthier. The zucchini noodles, also known as 'zoodles', are a great alternative to traditional pasta and make the meal significantly lighter. Remember, cooking is about having fun, so feel free to adjust the spice level to your liking! And if you want to save time spiralizing the zucchini, most grocery stores sell pre-spiralized packages.

Zesty Citrus Salmon fillets with Crispy Asparagus Spears

SERVINGS: 2	COOKING TIME: 20 MIN	CALORIES: 450

Ingredients

For the main dish:
- 2 salmon fillets
(200 g or 7 oz each)
- 1 tbsp olive oil (15 ml)
- Salt and pepper to taste
- Zest and juice of 1 lemon
- 2 cloves of garlic, minced

For the side dish:
- 20 asparagus spears
(500 g or 1.1 lbs)
- 1 tbsp olive oil (15 ml)
- Salt and pepper to taste
- 1 tsp garlic powder (5 g)

ADD SAVORY SNACKLETS

BUFFALO CAULIFLOWER WINGS:
Toss cauliflower florets with buffalo sauce
and a bit of oil. Air fry at 360°F (182°C) for
15-20 minutes, until crispy. These are great
for enjoying the flavors of buffalo wings but
with a vegetarian twist.

Directions

1. Start by patting the salmon fillets dry and season them with salt and pepper.

2. Drizzle olive oil over the salmon and rub it in to ensure it's fully coated.

3. Sprinkle the minced garlic, lemon zest and lemon juice over the salmon. Make sure the salmon is well coated and then place it in the air fryer basket.

4. Rinelly and dry the asparagus spears. Drizzle them with olive oil and season with salt, pepper and garlic powder.

5. Arrange the asparagus spears in the air fryer around the salmon fillets.

6. Set the air fryer to cook at 375°F (190°C) for 10 minutes.

7. After 10 minutes, check the salmon and asparagus. If needed, cook for an additional 2-3 minutes or until the salmon is cooked to your liking and the asparagus is crispy.

This meal is not just quick and delicious - it's also super healthy. Salmon is a terrific source of omega-3 fatty acids which are great for heart health, while asparagus offers a good dose of fiber, vitamins A, C, E and K. The zesty citrus flavor not only gives the salmon a flavorful kick, but the lemon also serves as a potent antioxidant. This is a low-carb, protein-rich and nutritious meal you can prepare in no time. Fun fact: did you know asparagus is known to boost your mood thanks to its high levels of folate and tryptophan? Now, who wouldn't want a mood-boosting side dish that's also delicious and healthy?

Crispy Air Fryer Fish Nuggets

SERVINGS: 2   COOKING TIME: 22 MIN   CALORIES: 200

Ingredients

- 1 pound (450 g) firm white fish fillets (such as cod, tilapia, or halibut)
- 1/2 cup all-purpose flour (60 g)
- 1 teaspoon paprika
- 1/2 teaspoon garlic powder
- Salt and black pepper to taste
- 2 large eggs, beaten
- 1 cup panko breadcrumbs (120 g)

ADD SAVORY SNACKLETS

COCONUT SHRIMP BITES:
Dip shrimp in beaten eggs, then roll in a mixture of shredded coconut and breadcrumbs. Air fry at 400°F (204°C) for about 8 minutes, flipping halfway through, until golden brown. Serve with a sweet chili sauce for dipping.

Directions

1. Prepare the Fish: Pat the fish fillets dry with paper towels and cut them into bite-sized nugget pieces.

2. Set Up Dredging Station: In a shallow dish, combine the flour, paprika, garlic powder, salt, and pepper. Place the beaten eggs in a second shallow dish. Put the panko breadcrumbs in a third shallow dish.

3. Coat the Fish: Dredge each fish piece first in the flour mixture, shaking off any excess. Dip next into the egg, allowing excess to drip off. Finally, coat thoroughly with panko breadcrumbs.

4. Cook the Fish Nuggets: Place the breaded fish nuggets in a single layer in the basket. Air fry for about 10-14 minutes, until the nuggets are golden brown and cooked through.

5. Serve hot with tartar sauce, ketchup, or your favorite dipping sauce.

Choosing the Right Fish: Firm white fish works best for nuggets as they hold together well and have a mild flavor that pairs beautifully with the crispy breadcrumb coating. Crispiness Tip: Ensure the fish nuggets are not crowded in the air fryer basket. Cooking in batches may be necessary depending on the size of your air fryer. Serving Suggestion: These fish nuggets are great for children and can be served as part of a healthy meal with some fresh salad or steamed vegetables.

Tangy Lemon-Garlic Shrimp and Vegetable Medley

SERVINGS: 2   COOKING TIME: 16MIN   CALORIES: 290

Ingredients

- - 1 lb (450 grams) of shrimp, deveined and shelled
- 2 medium-sized zucchinis, sliced
- 2 red bell peppers, sliced
- 2 tablespoons of olive oil
- 4 cloves of garlic, minced
- 1 lemon, juiced
- Salt and pepper to taste

ADD TASTY BITES

GARLIC PARMESAN ASPARAGUS:
Trim the woody ends off the asparagus. Toss the spears with olive oil, minced garlic, salt, and pepper. Arrange in a single layer in the air fryer basket. Cook at 400°F (204°C) for about 7-8 minutes, depending on the thickness of the asparagus. Once cooked, sprinkle generously with grated Parmesan cheese and serve immediately.

Directions

1. In a large bowl, toss shrimp, zucchinis, and red peppers with olive oil, minced garlic, and lemon juice.

2. Season with salt and pepper.

3. Arrange the shrimp and vegetables in a single layer in the air fryer basket. For optimal cooking, place shrimp at the bottom and layer the vegetables on top.

4. Set the air fryer to 400°F (200°C) and cook for 8 minutes.

5. Check the food, give a gentle stir to ensure even cooking, then cook for another 4-6 minutes until the shrimps are pink and vegetables are tender.

6. Serve immediately.

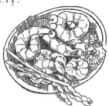

This Tangy Lemon-Garlic Shrimp and Vegetable Medley is not only a feast for the eyes but also a nutritional powerhouse loaded with protein and fiber. The zesty lemon pairs perfectly with seafood, and the garlic adds a depth of flavor you won't forget. With such bold tastes, you won't even notice that it's a low-calorie meal. Plus, here's a fun fact: Did you know shrimps can swim backward? While they are busy backpedaling in ocean waves, we are enjoying their wonderful taste in our supper plates!

Delightful Fish Tacos with Crunchy Coleslaw

SERVINGS: 2   COOKING TIME: 20 MIN   CALORIES: 435

Ingredients

- 2 large Tilapia Fillets
- 2 tablespoons Olive Oil
- 1 teaspoon Chili Powder
- 1 teaspoon Cumin
- 1 teaspoon Paprika
- ½ teaspoon Salt, plus extra for seasoning
- ¼ teaspoon Black Pepper
- 1 cup shredded Cabbage
- 1 medium Carrot, shredded
- ¼ cup finely chopped Onion
- 1 tablespoon Apple Cider Vinegar
- 2 tablespoons Mayonnaise
- 4-6 Corn Tortillas, depending on size and preference

Directions

1. To start, mix chili powder, cumin, paprika, salt, and olive oil in a bowl. Add the tilapia fillets and ensure they are fully coated.

2. Arrange the fillets in the air fryer in a single layer, avoiding overlap.

3. In the meantime, prepare the coleslaw by mixing the shredded cabbage, carrot, onion, apple cider vinegar, mayonnaise, salt, and black pepper in a bowl.

4. Cook the fish using the air fryer at 390F (200C) for 10 minutes,.

5. Warm up the tortillas in the air fryer for 2 minutes.

6. To assemble the fish tacos, flake the tilapia onto the tortillas and top with the crunchy coleslaw.

These Delightful Fish Tacos with Crunchy Coleslaw are a speedy dinner ideal for busy weeknights. The tilapia gives you high-quality protein and omega-3 fatty acids, while the coleslaw provides a fiber-kick and adds a refreshing crunch. Moreover, the use of spices in this recipe offers an optimal flavor burst without adding extra fat or calories. Fun Fact: Did you know that several studies have shown that eating fish may improve brain health? So, not only are these tacos quick, easy, and tasty, but they might just make you a little bit smarter, too!

Air Fryer Fish Cutlets

SERVINGS: 2   COOKING TIME: 20-25 MIN   CALORIES: 350

Ingredients

- Fish fillet (any kind, skinless and boneless) - 800g
- Zucchini - 140-200g
- Carrot - 60-80g
- Onion - 120-160g
- Salt, to taste
- Spices, to taste
- Eggs - 2 medium
- Coconut oil for greasing

ADD SAVORY SNACKLETS

MOZZARELLA STICKS:
Wrap mozzarella in wonton wrappers, brush with a little oil, and air fry at 375°C (190°C) for 6-8 minutes until crispy and golden. Dip in marinara sauce for a quick and easy appetizer.

Directions

1. Finely chop the fish fillets, zucchini, carrot, and onion, or use a food processor for a finer texture.

2. In a large bowl, combine the chopped ingredients with salt, spices, and beaten eggs. Mix until well combined.

3. Form the mixture into small patties. Ensure they are not too thick so they can cook evenly in the air fryer.

4. Preheat the air fryer to 180°C (356°F).

5. Lightly grease the air fryer basket with coconut oil. Place the cutlets in a single layer in the basket, ensuring they do not overlap.

6. Cook for 10-12 minutes, then flip the cutlets and cook for an additional 10-13 minutes or until they are golden brown and cooked through.

7. Serve hot with a side of your choice, such as a refreshing salad or tartar sauce.

- Adjust cooking times based on the size and thickness of the cutlets.

- You can replace coconut oil with any other preferred oil suitable for high heat.

- Ensure that the cutlets are not overcrowded in the air fryer to allow for even cooking.

- For extra crispiness, you can lightly coat the cutlets with breadcrumbs before cooking, keeping in mind this will alter the calorie count.

Crispy and Zesty Lemon-Parsley Cod with Sweet Potato Fries

SERVINGS: 2   COOKING TIME: 20 MIN   CALORIES: 450

Ingredients

For the main course:

- 2 Cod fillets (450 grams or 1 pound)
- Juice of 1 lemon
- 2 cloves of garlic, minced
- Handful of fresh parsley, finely chopped (about 4 tablespoons)
- Salt and pepper to taste

For the side dish:

- 2 large sweet potatoes (approx. 500 grams or 1.1 pounds), cut into fries
- 1 tablespoon of olive oil
- 1/2 tablespoon of smoked paprika
- Salt and pepper to taste

ADD SAVORY SNACKLETS

BANANA CHIPS:

Slice bananas thinly, sprinkle with a little cinnamon and sugar, and air fry at 350°F (177°C) for about 10 minutes until crisp. These banana chips are a healthy alternative to store-bought snacks and perfect for on-the-go munching.

Directions

1. Season the cod fillets with the lemon juice, minced garlic, chopped parsley, and salt and pepper.

2. Place the sweet potatoes in a bowl and drizzle the olive oil over them. Toss until all fries are covered, then sprinkle them with the smoked paprika, salt, and pepper.

3. Lay the sweet potato fries in a single layer in the air fryer. Use a cooking rack if necessary to avoid overcrowding fries.

4. Place the cod fillets on top of the fries for optimal steaming.

5. Cook at 400°F or 200°C for about 10-12 minutes.

6. Check if the fries and the fish are done. The fries should be crispy and the fish should be white and flaky.

7. If not, cook for an additional 3-5 minutes or until they meet the described criteria.

8. Once everything's cooked, serve the dish with a squeeze of fresh lemon juice over the top for additional zest.

This dish is a win-win for taste and health. Cod is a lean source of protein that's low in fat but high in vitamins and minerals. Not only that, but preparing it in an air fryer allows us to cut back on unnecessary oils and fats, keeping your dinner light and digestible. Plus, sweet potatoes are a rich source of fiber, vitamins, and antioxidants. The combination of zesty, garlic-lemon cod and smoky, sweet potato fries is sure to make your weekday dining a delightful experience. And here's a fun fact: Did you know that cod and parsley are a classic pairing in many European cuisines? Now, you can bring that tradition right into your home! Enjoy!

Zesty Lemon Pepper Tilapia with Crunchy Brussels Sprouts

SERVINGS: 2   COOKING TIME: 20 MIN   CALORIES: 320

Ingredients

Main Dish:
- 2 Tilapia fillets (1 pound / 450 grams)
- 1 tablespoon of Olive oil (15 ml)
- 1 tablespoon of Lemon zest (15 ml)
- 1 teaspoon of Black pepper (5 ml)
- 1/2 teaspoon of Salt (2.5 ml)

Side Dish:
- 2 cups of Brussels sprouts, halved (16 ounces / 450 grams)
- 2 tablespoons of Olive oil (30 ml)
- 1/2 teaspoon of Salt (2.5 ml)
- 1/2 teaspoon of Cracked black pepper (2.5 ml)

ADD SAVORY SNACKLETS

GREEK FETA BITES:
Mix crumbled feta with chopped spinach, dill, and a bit of lemon zest. Form into small patties and air fry at 360°F (182°C) for about 8 minutes until golden and firm. Enjoy a burst of Mediterranean flavors

Directions

1. Begin by gathering all your ingredients.

2. Pat the Tilapia fillets dry and rub each fillet with olive oil.

3. Sprinkle the lemon zest, black pepper, and salt evenly over each Tilapia fillet.

4. Place the Tilapia fillets in the air fryer tray.

5. In a bowl, toss the halved Brussels sprouts with olive oil, salt, and pepper.

6. Place the prepared Brussels sprouts in the air fryer tray above the Tilapia fillets.

7. Set the temperature of the air fryer to 400°F (200°C) and cook for 10 minutes.

8. After 10 minutes, carefully open the air fryer and flip the Tilapia fillets and Brussels sprouts.

9. Continue cooking for another 7-10 minutes until the Tilapia is cooked through and the Brussels sprouts are golden and crispy.

Seared to perfection, this Zesty Lemon Pepper Tilapia is a fantastic source of lean protein that pairs beautifully with our fiber-rich Crunchy Brussels Sprouts. The air fryer method locks in juices and flavors, delivering a wholesome, nutrient-packed meal in record time! Fun fact: Tilapia is not only tasty, but also packed with Omega-3 fatty acids which are great for heart health. The lemon zest adds a delightful tang, cutting through the earthiness of the Brussels sprouts for a balanced flavor profile. Enjoy this simple but delicious meal that only takes 20 minutes from start to finish. Perfect for a quick and healthy dinner!

Herbal Crusted Salmon and Zesty Citrus Salad

SERVINGS: 2   COOKING TIME: 20 MIN   CALORIES: 350

Ingredients

For the Main Dish:

- Two salmon fillets, 6 ounces each (170 grams)
- 1 tablespoon olive oil (15 ml)
- 1 tablespoon fresh thyme, finely chopped (1.8 grams)
- 1 tablespoon fresh rosemary, finely chopped (2 grams)
- Salt and pepper to taste

For the Side Dish:

- 2 large oranges, peeled and sliced (approximately 340 grams)
- 1 large fennel bulb, thinly sliced (about 250 grams)
- 1/4 cup fresh mint leaves, chopped (10 grams)
- 1 tablespoon olive oil (15 ml)
- Salt and pepper to taste

Directions

1. Brush salmon fillets evenly with the olive oil and season with salt and pepper.

2. Sprinkle the thyme and rosemary evenly over the fillets, pressing gently to adhere the herbs to the fish.

3. Place the seasoned salmon fillets into the air fryer, making sure they don't overlap.

4. Set the air fryer to 400°F (200°C) and cook the salmon for 10-12 minutes, until the fillets are flaky and cooked through.

5. While the salmon is cooking, combine the sliced oranges, fennel, and chopped mint in a large bowl.

6. Drizzle the salad with the olive oil, season with salt and pepper, and toss gently to combine.

7. Divide the citrus salad between two plates, top each with a salmon fillet, and serve immediately for a fresh, healthy dinner ready in just 20 minutes.

This Herbal Crusted Salmon and Zesty Citrus Salad recipe is the perfect quick, healthy, yet indulgent dinner for two you've been looking for. With protein-rich salmon, and a refreshing salad packed with vitamin C from the oranges and dietary fiber from the fennel, it's a meal that supports a balanced, healthy lifestyle. Plus, did you know? Salmon is a powerhouse of Omega-3 fatty acids, which boost heart health and improve cognitive function. Enjoy this meal knowing you're treating your body right!

Spicy Honey Glazed Salmon with Crispy Asparagus & Quinoa

SERVINGS: 2   **COOKING TIME: 20 MIN**   **CALORIES: 490**

Ingredients

For the Main Dish:

2 salmon fillets (6 ounces each)

1 tbsp of honey (14g / 0.5 oz)

1 tsp of chili powder (5g / 0.18 oz)

Salt to taste

For the Fiber-Rich Side Dishes:

15 asparagus spears

1 tsp of olive oil (5ml / 0.17 fl oz)

1/2 tsp of garlic powder (2.5g / 0.09 oz)

Salt and pepper to taste

1 cup of cooked quinoa (186g / 6.53 oz)

ADD SAVORY SNACKLETS

GARLIC PARMESAN BRUSSEL SPROUTS:
Halve Brussel sprouts and toss with olive oil, minced garlic, grated Parmesan, salt, and pepper. Air fry at 375°F (190°C) for about 12 minutes, shaking halfway through. Serve these crispy veggies as a healthy side dish or snack

Directions

1. Mix together honey, chili powder, and salt in a bowl.

2. Brush the mixture over the salmon fillets evenly.

3. Place the salmon fillets in the air fryer basket and cook at 375°F (190°C) for 7 minutes.

For the Asparagus:

4. Toss the asparagus spears in olive oil, garlic powder, salt, and pepper.

5. Arrange the spears in the air fryer beside the salmon.

6. Continue cooking the salmon and asparagus for another 5-7 minutes until the salmon is cooked through and the asparagus is crispy.

7. Serve the salmon and asparagus with cooked quinoa on the side.

This dish brings in a delightful fusion of flavors. The salmon offers omega-3 fatty acids, making it a top choice for a heart-healthy protein. Plus, it's topped with a sweet and spicy honey glaze that adds a beautiful caramelization and a mouthful of flavor. Our fiber-rich side dish, asparagus, not only adds a satisfying crunch but also is a great source of vitamins A, C, and K. Let's not forget it is air fried, ensuring it maintains all its nutritional value while achieving a crispy texture. Quinoa adds a grainy component to the dish, it's high in protein and makes this meal even more fulfilling. This meal is more than just delicious and quick; it has a balance of protein, fiber, and healthy fats, making it a perfect dinner option for those aiming to maintain a healthy lifestyle.

Quick'n'Easy Lemon Pepper Cod and Roasted Veggies

SERVINGS: 2   COOKING TIME: 20 MIN   CALORIES: 370

Ingredients

- 2 cod fillets - 8 ounces each (225 grams each)
- 2 teaspoon of lemon pepper spice
- 1 lemon, juiced
- 2 tablespoon of olive oil (30 ml)
- Salt to taste
- Fresh dill, chopped

Side Dish Ingredients:
- 1 large sweet potato (300 grams), cubed
- 1 cup of Brussels sprouts (150 grams), trimmed and halved
- 2 cloves of garlic, minced
- 1 tablespoon of olive oil (15 ml)

ADD SAVORY SNACKLETS

CHEDDAR JALAPEÑO CORNBREAD BITES:
Prepare your favorite cornbread batter, adding shredded cheddar and diced jalapeños. Pour into mini muffin tins and air fry at 350°F (177°C) for 10 minutes. These spicy bites are great for breakfast or as a side with chili.

Directions

1. Start by patting dry your cod fillets. Sprinkle them evenly with lemon pepper spice, salt, and add the fresh lemon juice. Allow it to marinate for about 10 minutes while you prepare your vegetables.

2. In a large bowl, toss your cubed sweet potato, halved Brussels sprouts, and minced garlic with 1 tablespoon of olive oil. Be sure every piece of vegetable is covered with the oil.

3. Put the vegetables in the air fryer basket first, creating an even layer at the bottom.

4. Next, place your marinated cod fillets on top of the vegetables. Drizzle 1 tablespoon olive oil evenly over the fish.

5. Set your air fryer to 400°F (200°C) and cook for about 12-15 minutes. Check in the last few minutes of cooking for desired crispness and to ensure the fish is cooked through.

Quick'n'Easy Lemon Pepper Air Fryer Cod and Roasted Veggies is a midweek savior! High in protein and rich in Omega-3 fatty acids, cod is a heart-healthy choice. The lemon pepper brings a zesty flavor, enhancing the freshness of the fish. The side of air-fried sweet potatoes and Brussels sprouts add a delightful crunch, and they're also packed with antioxidants and fiber, beneficial for a balanced diet. A great option for seafood lovers, this dish can be served with a fresh and simple salad to complete the meal. The best part? All of this wholesome goodness is cooked in an air fryer, enabling you to enjoy a nutritious dinner minus the fat.

Tangy Lemon Herb Haddock and Crispy Green Beans

SERVINGS: 2   COOKING TIME: 20 MIN   CALORIES: 350

Ingredients

For the Haddock:
- 1 lb (450 grams) Haddock fillets
- Juice of 1 lemon
- 2 tbsp (30 ml) Olive oil
- Salt and pepper to taste
- 1 tsp (5 ml) Dried herbs such as thyme, tarragon, or your choice

For the Green Beans:
- 1/2 lb (250 grams) Fresh green beans, trimmed
- 1 tbsp (15 ml) Olive oil
- Garlic powder to taste
- Fresh cracked black pepper to taste

ADD SAVORY SNACKLETS

GARLIC PARMESAN BRUSSEL SPROUTS: Halve Brussel sprouts and toss with olive oil, minced garlic, grated Parmesan, salt, and pepper. Air fry at 375°F (190°C) for about 12 minutes, shaking halfway through. Serve these crispy veggies as a healthy side dish or snack.

Directions

1. Brush both sides of each haddock fillet with olive oil and season with salt, pepper, and dried herbs of your choice.

2. Place the prepared haddock fillets in the air fryer basket and cook at 400°F (200°C) for 10 minutes.

3. While your fish cooks, toss your fresh green beans in olive oil and season with garlic powder and black pepper.

4. Once the fish has cooked, remove from the air fryer and keep warm. Place the seasoned green beans in the air fryer basket. Cook at 375°F (190°C) for 7-10 minutes until they reach your desired level of crispiness.

5. Serve the haddock hot with a squeeze of fresh lemon juice, alongside a helping of crispy green beans. Enjoy your quick, healthy dinner!

The Tangy Lemon Herb Haddock is not only packed with essential proteins but also provides an array of omega-3 fatty acids, which are known for their cardiovascular benefits. Adding the lemon juice enhances the fish's natural flavors while aiding in digestion. The Crispy Air Fryer Green Beans, on the other hand, up this dish's nutritional value by providing your necessary dietary fiber intake, making this a well-rounded, light, and healthy dinner. Enjoy with your partner on a cozy evening, and don't worry about the washing up, because using the air fryer keeps that to a minimum!

74

Lemon-Dill Air Fryer Salmon Pairs with Sweet Potato Fries

SERVINGS: 2   COOKING TIME: 20 MIN   CALORIES: 470

Ingredients

For the salmon:
- Two 6-ounce fillets of fresh salmon (170 grams each)
- 1 tablespoon of olive oil (15 ml)
- Juice of half a lemon (approximately 15 ml)
- 1 teaspoon of dried dill (5 grams)
- Salt and black pepper to taste

For the sweet potato fries:
- 2 medium sweet potatoes, peeled and cut into fries (approximately 400 grams)
- 1 tablespoon of olive oil (15 ml)
- 1/2 teaspoon of smoked paprika (2.5 grams)
- Salt and black pepper to taste

ADD SAVORY SNACKLETS

VEGETABLE SPRING ROLLS:
Stuff spring roll wrappers with a mix of shredded carrots, cabbage, and thinly sliced bell peppers. Brush lightly with oil and air fry at 400°F (204°C) for about 8 minutes, until crispy. Dip in soy sauce or sweet and sour sauce for a tasty treat.

Directions

1. Rub the salmon fillets with olive oil, lemon juice, dried dill, salt, and black pepper. Set aside to marinate for a few minutes.

2. Meanwhile, place the chopped sweet potatoes in a bowl, add olive oil, smoked paprika, salt, and pepper, and toss until evenly coated.

3. Arrange the sweet potato fries in the air fryer basket, ensuring they are not overlapping. Place the salmon fillets on top of them.

4. Cook everything together at 400°F (200°C) for 10 minutes.

5. After 10 minutes, remove the salmon fillets and shake the basket to ensure the fries cook evenly.

6. Return the salmon fillets to the air fryer and cook for another 5 to 7 minutes, or until the salmon is cooked through and the fries are golden brown and crispy.

This recipe is a wonderful healthy dinner for two. It's a high-protein, high-fiber meal that's sure to satisfy your hunger. The salmon's healthy fats are perfect for a heart-friendly diet, while the sweet potatoes give you a dose of fiber and essential vitamins. Plus, using an air fryer keeps the calories low while still creating a deliciously crispy texture. Mediterranean-inspired flair to the salmon, transporting your taste buds to sunny coasts right from the comfort of your kitchen. A fun bonus: sweet potatoes are one of the few vegetables that increase in nutritional value when cooked, meaning this dish really maximizes the goodness in your meal!

Herb Cod with Vegetable Medley in Air Fryer

SERVINGS: 2   COOKING TIME: 20 MIN   CALORIES: 390

Ingredients

- 2 cod fillets
(8 ounces each; 450 grams)
- 1 tablespoon of olive oil
(about 15 ml)
- 1 lemon, zested and juiced
- 2 cloves of garlic, minced
- 1 tablespoon of mixed dried herbs, such as thyme, rosemary and oregano
(15 grams)
- Salt and pepper to taste

For the Vegetable Medley:
- 1 bell pepper, cut into thin strips (150 grams)
- 1 zucchini, sliced into rounds
(200 grams)
- 1 red onion, thinly sliced
(160 grams)
- 1 tablespoon of olive oil (about 15 ml)
- Salt and pepper to taste

Directions

1. Rinse the cod fillets and pat them dry. Rub them with olive oil, lemon zest, minced garlic, mixed herbs, salt, and pepper.

2. In a large bowl, combine the bell pepper, zucchini, and red onion. Drizzle with olive oil, add salt and pepper, and toss to coat.

3. Lay the cod fillets in the air fryer basket. Surround them with the mixed vegetables, ensuring they don't overlap with the fillets.

4. Cook at 400°F (200°C) for about 10 minutes. Then, quickly open the air fryer and flip the cod fillets and the vegetables. Continue cooking for another 5–7 minutes, or until the cod is cooked through and the vegetables are tender.

5. Drizzle the cod with fresh lemon juice before serving.

This dish is the perfect blend of light protein and fiber-filled veggies. The clean, mild taste of the cod is excellently enhanced by the tart lemon, aromatic herbs, and flavorful vegetables, offering a healthy, balanced meal. One serving provides a good amount of lean protein, vitamin C, and fiber. Moreover, cooking in an air fryer requires less oil, keeping this meal low in calories and fat. Isn't it amazing that this delightful dinner takes only 20 minutes to prepare in your air fryer? So let's feel healthier and happier by giving our nutrition a convenient, flavor-loaded upgrade with this recipe!

Crispy Fish Fillets with a Side of Sweet Potato Fries and Crunchy Salad

SERVINGS: 2   COOKING TIME: 20 MIN   CALORIES: 325

Ingredients

- 2 medium hake fillets, about 140 gm each (9.882 oz each)
- 1/8 cup of olive oil (30 ml)
- Salt and black pepper to taste
- 1 medium sweet potato, cut into fries (about 200 grams or 7 oz)
- 1 cup mixed salad greens (about 40 grams or 1.4 oz)
- 2 tablespoons of lemon juice (30 ml)
- 1 tablespoon of honey (15 ml)

ADD SAVORY SNACKLETS

MOZZARELLA AND HERB MELTS:
Place slices of mozzarella cheese on small pieces of ciabatta or baguette, sprinkle with dried Italian herbs, and a touch of garlic powder. Air fry at 360°F (182°C) for about 3-5 minutes until the cheese is melted and bubbly. Serve these cheesy melts as a warm and comforting snack.

Directions

1. Start by seasoning your hake fillets with olive oil, salt and pepper. Allow them to rest for a few minutes to absorb the flavors.

2. While your fish is marinating, slice the sweet potato into fries. Lightly coat them with some olive oil and sprinkle them with salt.

3. Place the seasoned fish fillets into the air fryer basket, ensure they're not overlapping.

4. Place the sweet potato fries above the fish fillets in the air fryer, allowing them to receive heat from both top and bottom.

5. Cook for around 15 minutes at 200°C (400 Fahrenheit), make sure to shake the fries after 8 minutes to ensure a uniform cook and a crispy finish.

6. Meanwhile, in a bowl, mix together the salad greens, lemon juice, honey for a simple, nutritious, and refreshing salad.

7. Once the fish and fries are done, serve them immediately with the crunchy side salad.

This dish offers a perfect balance of proteins, carbs, and fibers, making it a healthy yet tasty option for quick dinners. The crispy fish and sweet potato fries cooked in the air fryer maintain their nutrients while providing that irresistible crunch. The raw salad doesn't only add color to the plate, it also provides freshness and texture. Do you know the beautiful flaky texture in fish is best achieved by air frying? This has been a chef's secret for years. Plus, the honey in the salad is not just for sweetness, it's packed with antioxidants which boost your overall health. Isn't that a fun fact to impress your dinner guest? Don't forget to enjoy this easy-to-make, nutritious, and tasty meal.

Crispy Baked Salmon with Garlic Green Beans and Carrot Fries

SERVINGS: 2   COOKING TIME: 20 MIN   CALORIES: 400

Ingredients

- For the Salmon:
- 2 skin-on salmon fillets (approximately 180g or 6oz each)
- 1 teaspoon olive oil (5ml)
- Salt and fresh ground black pepper to taste
- 1/2 lemon juice and zest

- For the Garlic Green Beans:
- 150g or 5oz fresh green beans
- 1 teaspoon olive oil (5ml)
- 2 cloves garlic, minced
- Salt and fresh ground black pepper to taste

- For the Carrot Fries:
- 2 large carrots (233 g)
- 1 teaspoon olive oil (5ml)
- Salt and fresh ground black pepper to taste

Directions

1. Set salmon fillets in the refrigerator to bring to room temperature. Rinse green beans and carrots and pat dry.
2. Cut the carrots into fry-like strips.
3. In a bowl, toss the carrot fries with 1 tsp olive oil, salt, and pepper.
4. Place the carrot fries in your air fryer basket evenly spread out. Cook at 380°F (190°C) for 10 minutes.
5. In the meantime, toss the green beans with garlic, 1 tsp olive oil, salt, and pepper.
6. After the carrot fries have cooked for 10 minutes, take out the air fryer basket. Give the carrot fries a shake before adding the green beans on the top. Continue to cook at 380°F (193°C) for another 5 minutes.
7. On a plate, pat the salmon fillets dry with a paper towel. Rub each fillet with 1 tsp of olive oil, salt, pepper, and the lemon zest.
8. Once the veggies are cooked, remove them from the air fryer and temporarily place them in a bowl. Now, arrange the salmon fillets skin-side-down in the basket with space around each to allow even cooking. Cook at 380°F (193°C) for the final 5 minutes or until your desired doneness.
9. Serve the air fried salmon with the carrot fries and garlic green beans, drizzled with lemon juice over the top.

This Crispy Baked Salmon with Garlic Green Beans and Carrot Fries is a wholesome and satisfying meal. The salmon is rich in heart-healthy omega-3 fatty acids and proteins, while carrots and green beans contribute fiber and essential vitamins. The crispiness of the air fried meal means enjoyable texture without excessive oil. The garlic in the green beans and the tangy burst from lemon on your salmon are sure to invigorate your taste buds. This recipe uses the air fryer to cook the vegetables and the fish separately, yet simultaneously. When you open the air fryer to add in new ingredients, the circulating heat remains pretty constant, so there's no 'preheating' required!

Baked Salmon with Lemon-Dill Yogurt Sauce and Sweet Potato Rounds

SERVINGS: 2   COOKING TIME: 20 MIN   CALORIES: 500

Ingredients

- 2 salmon fillets
  (14oz / 400g)
- 2 sweet potatoes
  (13oz / 370g)
- 3 tablespoons olive oil (45ml)
- 1 tablespoon of lemon juice (15ml)
- 1/2 cup Greek yogurt (120ml)
- 1 teaspoon dried dill (5ml)
- Salt and pepper to taste

ADD SAVORY SNACKLETS

MINI FRITTATA CUPS

Simply whisk together 4 large eggs, 1/4 cup of milk, salt, and pepper, then stir in 1/2 cup of shredded cheese and 1/2 cup of diced vegetables like bell peppers, onions, and spinach. Optionally, add diced ham or bacon for extra flavor. Pour the mixture into greased silicone muffin cups, place in the air fryer, and cook at 350°F (175°C) for about 12-15 minutes until the frittatas are puffed and set. These delightful mini frittatas are perfect for a grab-and-go meal or a protein-rich snack, easy to customize and deliciously satisfying.

Directions

1. Rinse the salmon fillets and pat dry with a paper towel. Drizzle each fillet lightly with a tablespoon of olive oil, and sprinkle with salt and pepper to taste. Now, place the salmon fillets into the air fryer basket.

2. Wash the sweet potatoes and cut them into 1/2 inch (1.27cm) rounds. In a bowl, lightly coat the sweet potato slices with the remaining olive oil and a pinch of salt.

3. Arrange the sweet potato slices around the salmon fillets in the air fryer basket.

4. Cook everything together in the air fryer at 350°F (175°C) for about 15 minutes, or until the salmon is cooked through and the sweet potatoes are soft and slightly caramelized.

5. While your dinner is cooking, prepare the lemon-dill yogurt sauce. In a bowl, combine the Greek yogurt, lemon juice, and dried dill. Stir until well combined.

6. Once the cooking time is up, serve the salmon and sweet potato rounds with a dollop of the lemon-dill yogurt sauce.

This dish offers a nutritious balance of protein from the salmon and fiber-rich carbs from the sweet potatoes. The lemon and dill yogurt sauce adds a fresh tanginess that enhances the salmon's flavor. The air fryer ensures a perfectly cooked salmon fillet that's juicy on the inside and deliciously crunchy on the outside. Sweet potatoes also benefit from the air fryer's high heat, developing a nice caramelized exterior that's full of flavor. A fun fact about sweet potatoes: they are high in beta-carotene, which converts to vitamin A in our bodies and helps to boost our immune system. Cook, enjoy, and stay healthy!

Fish in Coconut-Almond Crust

SERVINGS: 2   **COOKING TIME: 15-18 MIN**   **CALORIES: 420**

Ingredients

- 200g cod fillet
- 1 cm cube of ginger, finely grated
- Zest and juice from 1 lime
- 1/4 tsp cayenne pepper
- 1/2 tsp black pepper
- 1/2 cup light coconut milk
- 300g white sea fish fillet
  (in addition to cod)
- 1 tsp salt
- 1 cup almond flour

ADD SAVORY SNACKLETS

PARMESAN ZUCCHINI COINS:
Slice zucchini into thick coins, dip in beaten egg, then coat in a mixture of grated Parmesan cheese and Italian seasoning. Air fry at 380°F (193°C) for about 10 minutes, flipping once, until crispy and golden. These make a great side dish or a healthy alternative to chips.

Directions

1. Preheat the air fryer to 200°C (390°F).
2. In a kitchen processor, combine the ginger, lime zest and juice, cayenne pepper, and black pepper. Blend until smooth.
3. Add the light coconut milk to the spice mixture in the processor and blend lightly to mix.
4. Pat the fish fillets dry with paper towels. If they are very large, cut them into smaller pieces suitable for two servings.
5. Dip each fish fillet into the coconut milk mixture to coat thoroughly, then dredge in the almond flour, pressing gently to help the crust adhere.
6. Place the crusted fish fillets in the air fryer basket. Make sure they do not touch each other for even cooking.
7. Cook for 15-18 minutes, or until the fish is cooked through and the crust is golden and crispy.
8. Serve immediately.

- Adjust the cooking time based on the thickness of the fish fillets.
- If your air fryer tends to cook foods quite crisply, you might consider spraying a little oil over the almond-crusted fish before cooking to enhance browning.
- This recipe can be served with a side of fresh salad or steamed vegetables for a balanced meal.

Mediterranean Vegetable Casserole with Quinoa and Grilled Halloumi Cheese

SERVINGS: 2   COOKING TIME: 18 MIN   CALORIES: 360

Ingredients

For the casserole -
- 1 cup of quinoa (185 grams)
- 2 cups of vegetable broth (500 ml)
- 1 zucchini, chopped (approx. 150 grams)
- 1 red bell pepper, chopped (approx. 150 grams)
- 2 cups of cherry tomatoes, halved (300 grams)
- 5 oz of halloumi cheese, sliced (140 grams)

For the side salad -
- 2 cups of arugula (60 grams)
- 1 cucumber, sliced (approx. 300 grams)
- Juice of one lemon

Directions

1. Rinse the quinoa under cold running water until the water runs clear.

2. Place the quinoa in the air fryer and cover it with the vegetable broth. Set the air fryer to 350°F (175°C) for 12 minutes.

3. While the quinoa is cooking, chop the zucchini and red bell pepper, and halve the cherry tomatoes.

4. When the quinoa is ready, add the chopped vegetables and halloumi slices on top of it and cook for another 5 minutes at 350°F (175°C).

5. While the casserole is cooking, prepare the side salad: wash the arugula, slice the cucumber, and mix them in a large bowl. Squeeze the lemon juice over it.

This Mediterranean Vegetable Casserole is a wonderful mixture of colors, tastes, and textures. It's high in fiber and includes a protein-rich quinoa and halloumi cheese that support the ideal of a healthy lifestyle.

Moreover, halloumi cheese might be scrumptious, but it's also high in protein and calcium. Interestingly, due to its high melting point, halloumi can easily be grilled or fried without losing its form - perfect for air frying!

The accompanying salad introduces a fresh, light component that complements the casserole wonderfully. Plus, did you know? Arugula, also known as 'rocket,' is not only delicious but is also packed with antioxidants. An ideal pair for this golden, crispy casserole!

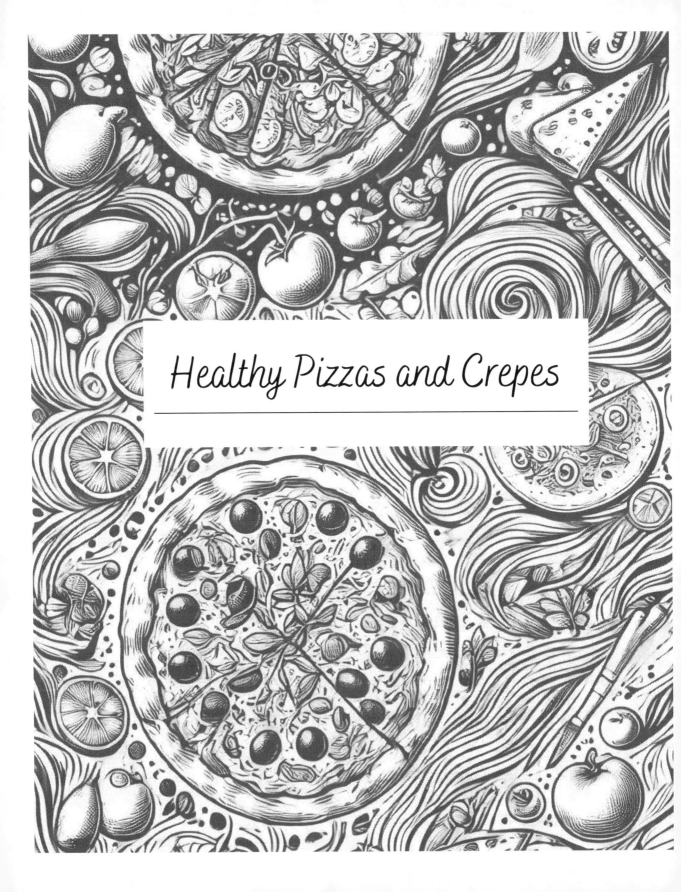

Healthy Pizzas and Crepes

Hearty Whole Wheat Air Fryer Pizza Base

SERVINGS: 2   COOKING TIME: 25 MIN   CALORIES: 180

Ingredients

Whole wheat flour (2 cups or 240 g)

Active dry yeast (1 packet or 2 1/4 teaspoons)

Sugar (1 teaspoon)

Warm water (1 cup or 240 mL, approximately 110°F or 43°C)

Olive oil (1 tablespoon plus extra for greasing)

Salt (1 teaspoon)

ACTIVATE THE YEAST:

In a small bowl, combine the warm water and sugar. Sprinkle the yeast over the top and let it sit for 5 to 10 minutes until it becomes frothy. This indicates that the yeast is active and ready to use.

PREPARE THE DOUGH:

In a large mixing bowl, combine the whole wheat flour and salt. Add the frothy yeast mixture along with 1 tablespoon of olive oil. Stir until the mixture forms a rough dough. Turn the dough out onto a floured surface and knead for about 8 to 10 minutes, or until smooth and elastic. Add a little extra flour if the dough is too sticky.

FIRST RISE:

Place the kneaded dough in a bowl greased with a bit of olive oil, turning the dough to coat it lightly in oil. Cover the bowl with a clean cloth or plastic wrap and let it rise in a warm, draft-free area for about 1 hour, or until doubled in size.

SHAPE AND PRE-BAKE THE BASE:

Once risen, punch down the dough to release any air bubbles. Roll the dough out into your desired pizza shape that can fit in your air fryer basket. Preheat the air fryer to 360°F (182°C). Place the shaped dough in the air fryer basket and pre-bake for 3-4 minutes on each side to set the shape and prevent sogginess.

You can store prepared pizza dough bases in the refrigerator, which is a convenient way to prepare in advance if you plan to use them within a few days. Here's how to properly store your pizza bases:

1. Prepare the Bases: After kneading and rolling out your dough into pizza bases, make sure they are evenly and thinly rolled for the best baking results.

2. Pre-bake (Optional): If you prefer, you can pre-bake the bases for about 3-4 minutes in an air fryer or oven at 360°F (182°C) to set the shape. This step helps prevent the bases from becoming soggy once you add toppings and bake them later.

3. Cool Down: Allow the bases to cool completely if they have been pre-baked. This prevents condensation from forming inside the packaging, which could make the dough soggy.

4. Wrap Properly: Wrap each base individually in plastic wrap or place them in airtight freezer bags. This helps to maintain freshness and prevents the dough from absorbing any odors from the refrigerator.

5. Refrigerate: Store the wrapped pizza bases in the refrigerator. Properly stored, they can last for up to 5 days.

6. Usage: When you're ready to use them, simply take a base out of the refrigerator, let it come to room temperature for a few minutes, add your toppings, and bake as desired. This method is excellent for managing meal times efficiently, allowing you to enjoy homemade pizza with minimal preparation on busy days.

This whole wheat pizza base is an excellent alternative for those seeking a healthier option. The air fryer offers a quick and energy-efficient method to bake the pizza, maintaining a crisp crust and evenly cooked toppings. Adjusting the cooking times slightly depending on the size and model of your air fryer. Enjoy creating your custom pizza with the added benefits of whole grains!

Crispy Veggie Heaven Pizza

SERVINGS: 2   COOKING TIME: 24 MIN   CALORIES: 350

Ingredients

- 1 whole wheat pizza base (150 grams)
2. 1/2 cup marinara sauce (125 ml)
- 1/2 cup reduced-fat shredded mozzarella cheese (50 grams)
- 1 cup bell pepper slices, assorted colors (150 grams)
- 1/2 cup thin-sliced mushrooms (75 grams)
- 1/2 cup fresh spinach leaves (15 grams)
7. 2 tablespoon olive oil (30 ml)
- 1/2 teaspoon dried oregano (1 gram)
- 1/2 teaspoon dried basil (1 gram)
- Salt and pepper to taste

ADD SAVORY SNACKLETS

MINI CAPRESE SKEWERS:
Thread a cherry tomato, a small ball of mozzarella, and a fresh basil leaf onto small skewers. Drizzle with balsamic glaze and a touch of olive oil. Air fry at 360°F (182°C) for just 2-3 minutes to warm through without melting the cheese completely. This quick dish offers a burst of fresh flavors.

Directions

1. Start by lightly brushing the whole wheat pizza base with 1 tablespoon of olive oil.
2. Spread the marinara sauce evenly on the pizza base, leaving some space for the crust.
3. Sprinkle the shredded mozzarella cheese over the sauce.
4. Arrange the bell pepper slices, sliced mushrooms, and fresh spinach leaves evenly on top of the cheese.
5. Drizzle the remaining tablespoon of olive oil over the vegetables and sprinkle dried oregano and basil on top.
6. Add salt and pepper to your taste preference.
7. Place the pizza in the air fryer on a single layer.
8. Cook for 10-12 minutes, or until the cheese is melted and crust is crispy. Make sure to rotate the pizza half-way through the cooking time.
9. Let it cool for a few minutes before slicing and serving.

This Pizza not only offers a quick and healthy dinner option, but it also provides a good balance of grains, protein, and vitamins from the veggies. The whole wheat pizza crust is a better source of fiber than white crust, and reduced-fat mozzarella gives the right amount of protein without overloading on calories. The medley of colorful vegetables not only gives this pizza a vibrant and appealing look, but they also pack this dish with essential nutrients. Cook up this dish on nights when you're tight on time, or simply when you want to treat yourself to some fast, homemade pizza.

Quick and Flavorful Chicken-Apple Pizza

SERVINGS: 2   COOKING TIME: 24 MIN   CALORIES: 450

Ingredients

- 1 healthy pizza base (18 cm /7 inches)
- 100 grams or ½ cup of marinara pizza sauce
- 175 grams or 1 cup cooked, shredded chicken
- 80 grams or 1/3rd cup mozzarella cheese
- 1 small apple, thinly sliced
- A handful of fresh basil
- 1 tablespoon of extra virgin olive oil

For the side:
- Mixed salad greens, preferably spinach and rocket (arugula)
- 1 tablespoon of balsamic vinaigrette also a pinch of salt and pepper to taste

ADD TASTY BITES

TERIYAKI MEATBALLS:
Combine ground beef or turkey with breadcrumbs, a beaten egg, minced garlic, and a splash of teriyaki sauce. Form into small meatballs and air fry at 380°F (190°C) for about 10-12 minutes until cooked through. Serve with extra teriyaki sauce for a flavorful bite-sized treat.

Directions

1. Start with spreading marinara sauce evenly on the pizza base or naan.

2. Sprinkle your shredded chicken all over the sauce, covering the surface of the naan or pizza base.

3. Then, distribute your thinly sliced apples all over the shredded chicken layer.

4. Finish this layering process by sprinkling mozzarella cheese on top.

5. Put your pizza into the air fryer and cook it at 375 degrees Fahrenheit / 190 degrees Celsius for 8 to 10 minutes, or until you see the cheese bubbling and turning golden.

6. While your pizza is cooking, toss your mixed salad greens with balsamic vinaigrette, salt, and pepper.

7. Once your pizza is done, carefully remove it from the air fryer, cut it into slices, and serve it immediately with your prepared salad on the side.

This Pizza is a beautiful blend of high-quality proteins from chicken, fibers from apples and whole grain pizza base, plus, it carries less fat as pizza is cooked in an air fryer which requires minimal oil. The slightly sweet crunch of apples contrasts exquisitely with the savory chicken and tangy marinara. The accompanying salad provides additional fiber helping you feel full and satisfied. The flavors and nutrients of this meal perfectly cater to a healthy lifestyle without sacrificing taste. Enjoy your speedy dinner! Because the family that eats together, stays together!

Chicken Margherita Pizza with Zucchini Fries

SERVINGS: 2   COOKING TIME: 24 MIN   CALORIES: 450

Ingredients

For the Pizza:
1 healthy pizza base, ready flatbread or naan (255g)
- 1 cup marinara or pizza sauce (240ml)
- 1.5 cups shredded mozzarella (170g)
- 1 grilled chicken breast, thinly sliced (100-120g)
- 1/2 cup fresh basil leaves (15g)
For the Zucchini Fries:
- 2 Medium zucchinis (400g)
- 1/2 cup bread crumbs (60g)
- 1/2 cup grated parmesan (50g)
- 1 tsp Italian seasoning (5ml)

ADD SAVORY SNACKLETS

SWEET AND SPICY CARROT FRIES:
Cut carrots into fry-shaped sticks, toss with a little olive oil, honey, and a pinch of chili powder. Air fry at 390°F (199°C) for 10-12 minutes, shaking halfway through until crispy. These carrot fries are a sweet and spicy alternative to traditional fries.

Directions

1. Spread marinara sauce evenly on your flatbread and sprinkle half of the mozzarella cheese over it.

2. Arrange chicken slices and scatter fresh basil leaves. Top it with the remaining mozzarella cheese.

3. Place the pizza in the air fryer and cook at 200°C or 390°F for 8-10 minutes, until the cheese is melted and slightly golden.

4. While the pizza cooks, slice zucchinis into sticks.

5. In a medium bowl, mix bread crumbs, parmesan, and Italian seasoning. Dip each zucchini stick in the mix and arrange on the air fryer rack.

6. After removing the pizza, cook the zucchini fries at 200°C or 390°F for 10 minutes, turning halfway through until crispy.

7. Remove and serve hot alongside the pizza.

This Chicken Margherita Pizza paired with Zucchini Fries makes for an undeniably delightful meal. The combination brings restaurant-quality food straight to your table, but in a healthier way thanks to our air fryer! Chicken is a great source of lean protein, and the zucchini fries are a fun way to add more vegetables to your meals. You'll enjoy a hearty dinner that's also balanced, light, and full of flavor. Did you know that basil is not just a tasty herb, but it also has compounds that have anti-inflammatory and antibacterial properties? Bon appétit!

Basil Pesto Pizza with Crispy Kale and Goat Cheese

SERVINGS: 2   COOKING TIME: 24 MIN   CALORIES: 300

Ingredients

For the Pizza:
- 1 thin premade healthy pizza base, ready flatbread or naan (14 ounces)
- 3 tablespoons pesto (45 grams)
- 1 cup goat cheese (150 grams)
- 1 cup sliced bell peppers (150 grams)
- 1 cup sliced fresh mushrooms (70 grams)
- 1 tablespoon olive oil (15 ml)

For the Crispy Kale:
- 2 cups roughly chopped kale (134 grams)
- 1 tablespoon olive oil (15 ml)
- Sea salt to taste

ADD SAVORY SNACKLETS

CRISPY AVOCADO FRIES:
Slice avocados into wedges, dip in beaten eggs, and coat with a mixture of panko breadcrumbs and Parmesan cheese. Air fry at 400°F (200°C) for 10 minutes, flipping halfway through until golden and crispy. Serve with a dipping sauce like spicy mayo or aioli.

Directions

1. Spread the pesto evenly over the pizza crust.

2. Sprinkle the goat cheese over the pesto.

3. Layer the bell peppers and mushrooms over the cheese.

4. Lightly brush the top of the pizza with olive oil.

5. Place the pizza in the air fryer. Set the temperature to 375°F (190°C) and cook for about 12 minutes.

6. While the pizza cooks, toss the kale with olive oil and sea salt.

7. After about 12 minutes in the air fryer, carefully remove the pizza and set it aside.

8. Add the kale to the air fryer and cook for 5 minutes until crispy.

9. Cut the cooked pizza into slices and serve hot with a side of crispy kale.

This Pizza recipe with Crispy Kale and Goat Cheese is perfect for those who love a good veggie-loaded dish. The pesto and goat cheese provide a beautiful richness to the lean, crisp vegetables, while the air fryer ensures a perfectly crisp crust every time. The crispy kale gets beautifully crunchy in the air fryer, serving as a healthful side that will have you craving for more. This recipe offers a wonderful source of fiber and antioxidants from all the delicious vegetables. Make this meal a weeknight favorite! But remember, the real secret is in the air-fryer that keeps everything crispy without the excess fat of traditional frying methods. What a delicious and nutritious way to end your day!

Zesty Mediterranean Garden Pizza

SERVINGS: 2   COOKING TIME: 24 MIN   CALORIES: 380

Ingredients

For the pizza:
- 1 whole wheat pizza base (approximately 12 inches in diameter)
- 35 grams (1.23 ounces) of turkey pepperoni
- 113 grams (4 ounces) of light mozzarella cheese, shredded
- 60 grams (2 ounces) of black olives, sliced
- 1 medium-sized bell pepper, sliced
- 1 medium-sized onion, thinly sliced
- 85 grams (3 ounces) of cherry tomatoes, halved
- 1 tablespoon of olive oil
- 1 tablespoon of dried oregano
- Salt and pepper to taste

For the side salad:
- 2 cups baby spinach
- 1 tablespoon of balsamic vinegar
- 1 tablespoon of olive oil
- Salt and pepper to taste

Directions

1. Using a kitchen brush, lightly coat the air fryer basket with olive oil.

2. Place the whole wheat pizza base on the oiled basket.

3. Layer the pizza with turkey pepperoni, shredded mozzarella, black olives, sliced bell pepper, onion, and cherry tomatoes.

4. Drizzle olive oil over the toppings and season with dried oregano, salt, and pepper.

5. Cook in the air fryer at 180°C (360°F) for 10 minutes or until the cheese has melted and the crust is crispy.

6. While the pizza cooks, assemble the salad. In a bowl, toss together baby spinach, balsamic vinegar, olive oil, salt, and pepper.

7. Serve the Zesty Mediterranean Garden Pizza with the side salad.

Sharing Mediterranean-inspired flavors, this pizza is laden with nutrient-rich vegetables and lean protein, making it a great choice for a quick, balanced dinner. The fiber-rich spinach salad on the side not only complements the flavors of the pizza but also boosts the nutrient profile of your meal. Without the need to preheat, the air fryer offers a speedy solution, delivering crisp, delicious pizza in a snap! Interesting fact: olives, found in our pizza, are a natural source of antioxidants. You can customize this recipe to your liking by swapping out or incorporating more of your favorite veggies. Happy air frying!

Super Green Lean-Mean Veggie Pizza

SERVINGS: 2   COOKING TIME: 24 MIN   CALORIES: 357

Ingredients

Main Ingredients:
- 1 medium-sized whole wheat pizza crust (about 12") or 150 grams
- 3/4 cup marinara sauce or 178 ml
- 1 cup shredded mozzarella cheese or 225 grams
- 1 cup shredded spinach or 30 grams
- 1/2 cup chopped bell peppers or 75 grams
- 1/2 cup chopped broccoli or 78 grams
- 1/4 cup diced onions or 40 grams
- 1/2 cup sliced tomatoes or 90 grams
- 1 tablespoon olive oil or 15 ml
- Salt and pepper to taste

Fiber-rich Side dish:
- 2 cups mixed green salad or 40 grams
- 1 tablespoon of low-fat vinaig

Directions

1. Start by brushing your whole wheat pizza crust evenly with your desired amount of olive oil.

2. Spread the marinara sauce over the crust, leaving a border for the crust.

3. Sprinkle the shredded mozzarella evenly over the sauce.

4. Distribute the spinach, bell peppers, broccoli, onions, and tomatoes over the bed of cheese.

5. Season lightly with salt and pepper.

6. Put your pizza in the basket or on the tray of your air fryer, then cook at 375°F or 190°C for 10 minutes or until the crust is crispy and cheese is melted and bubbly.

7. While the pizza is cooking, toss the mixed greens with the vinaigrette for your side salad.

8. Once the pizza is done, let it cool for a few minutes before cutting into slices.

Our Super Green Lean-Mean Veggie Pizza is more than just another pizza; it's a ticket to a healthier lifestyle. Its variety of vegetables provide plenty of vital vitamins and minerals, while the whole wheat crust adds an extra punch of fiber. The homemade marinara sauce cuts down on preservatives and the excess sugar found in store brands. Plus, the side salad is not just to add color to your plate, it comes packed with fiber, vitamin K, vitamin C, and folate. Delicious and nutritious, this recipe ensures that you do not have to choose between taste and health. The air fryer's magic comes into play to give you a crispy pizza without the grease in just 20 minutes. Thursday is no longer the only pizza night; any night can be with this healthful spin on an all-time favorite dish!

Cheese Tortilla in 20 Minutes

SERVINGS: 2   **COOKING TIME: 20 MIN**   **CALORIES: 450**

Ingredients

- Milk: 160 g
- Egg: 2 pcs
- Corn flour: 90 g
- Cheese (15–20% fat), grated: 100 g
- Salt, pepper, greens: to taste
- Optional ingredients: sliced avocado, fresh salsa, shredded cheese, cooked meats, assorted vegetables, beans, sauces, fresh herbs, sliced olives, and lime wedges.

ADD SAVORY SNACKLETS

ZUCCHINI PARMESAN CRISPS:
Slice zucchini into thin rounds and dip each slice into beaten eggs, then dredge in a mixture of Parmesan cheese and breadcrumbs. Air fry at 390°F (200°C) for about 10 minutes, until crispy and golden. These crisps are a healthy alternative to potato chips and are wonderfully addictive.

Directions

1. Prepare the tortilla batter by mixing milk, eggs, and corn flour in a bowl until smooth.

2. Add grated cheese to the mixture along with salt, pepper, and greens according to taste, and mix well.

3. Pour half of the batter into the silicon flat form, trying to spread it out to cover the bottom or to the fryer basket. You can use two silicone molds or metal rings at once by placing the second one on the rack above the first. This way, you will get two tortillas ready at the same time.

4. Cook for 7 minutes, then carefully flip the tortilla using a spatula, and cook for another 7-10 minutes or until golden brown and crispy. To make it even more crispy, take it out of the mold and cook it on the rack.

5. Repeat steps 4 and 5 for the remaining batter.

6. You can complement your tortilla with ingredients like sliced avocado, fresh salsa, shredded cheese, cooked meats, a variety of vegetables, beans, sauces like sour cream or hummus, fresh herbs, olives, and lime wedges for added flavor.

7. Serve hot.

- Adjust cooking times slightly based on your air fryer model and desired crispiness.
- For added flavor, you can sprinkle some extra cheese on top halfway through the cooking time.

Zucchini Mozzarella Pancakes

SERVINGS: 2   **COOKING TIME: 25 MIN**   **CALORIES:180**

Ingredients

- 2 Zucchini (medium-sized)
- 4 Eggs
- Mozzarella cheese, 60g
- Cornstarch, 2 tsp
- Salt, to taste
- Black pepper, to taste

ADD SAVORY SNACKLETS

STUFFED DATES:

Pit dates and stuff each one with a mixture of cream cheese and chopped walnuts. Wrap each date with a small slice of bacon and secure with a toothpick. Air fry at 370°F (188°C) for 6-8 minutes or until the bacon is crispy. These sweet and savory bites are a decadent treat

Directions

1. Grate the zucchinis and squeeze out the excess water as much as possible.

2. In a bowl, mix the grated zucchini with beaten eggs, cornstarch, salt, and pepper until well incorporated.

3. Preheat the air fryer to 380°F (190°C).

4. Form the mixture into two individual pancake shapes on parchment paper small enough to fit in the air fryer basket.

5. Place the parchment paper with the pancakes in the air fryer basket and cook for 12 minutes or until the edges are golden and crispy.

6. Sprinkle half of the mozzarella cheese on each pancake and make a small well in the center. Crack one egg into each well carefully.

7. Return to the air fryer and cook for an additional 5-7 minutes, or until the egg whites are set but yolks are still slightly runny.

8. Carefully remove from the air fryer and serve hot.

Make sure to squeeze the grated zucchini well to avoid excess moisture; this helps in getting a crispier texture.
Cooking times may vary slightly depending on your specific air fryer model.
This meal is great for a low-carb diet and can be enjoyed any time of the day.

Dietary Zucchini Pancake "Hachapuri"

SERVINGS: 2   **COOKING TIME: 24 MIN**   **CALORIES: 195**

Ingredients

- 2 Zucchini (medium-sized)
- 4 Eggs
- Mozzarella cheese, 60g
- Cornstarch, 2 tsp
- Salt, to taste
- Black pepper, to taste

 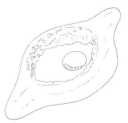

ADD SAVORY SNACKLETS

SPICY TUNA STUFFED PEPPERS:
Mix canned tuna with mayonnaise, sriracha, and chopped scallions. Slice mini bell peppers in half and remove the seeds, then stuff them with the tuna mixture. Air fry at 370°F (188°C) for about 10 minutes or until the peppers are tender. These are great for a quick and healthy protein-packed snack.

Directions

1. Grate the zucchinis and squeeze out the excess water as much as possible.

2. In a bowl, mix the grated zucchini with beaten eggs, cornstarch, salt, and pepper until well incorporated.

3. Preheat the air fryer to 380°F (190°C).

4. Form the mixture into two individual pancake shapes on parchment paper small enough to fit in the air fryer basket.

5. Place the parchment paper with the pancakes in the air fryer basket and cook for 12 minutes or until the edges are golden and crispy.

6. Sprinkle half of the mozzarella cheese on each pancake and make a small well in the center. Crack one egg into each well carefully.

7. Return to the air fryer and cook for an additional 5-7 minutes, or until the egg whites are set but yolks are still slightly runny.

8. Carefully remove from the air fryer and serve hot.

Make sure to squeeze the grated zucchini well to avoid excess moisture; this helps in getting a crispier texture.

Cooking times may vary slightly depending on your specific air fryer model.

This meal is great for a low-carb diet and can be enjoyed any time of the day.

Oat Crepe

SERVINGS: 2   **COOKING TIME: 20 MIN**   **CALORIES: 250-300**

Ingredients

- 6 tablespoons of oat flour or oat flakes blended to a powder
- 2 eggs
- 1/3 cup (80 ml) of milk or kefir
- A pinch of salt

ADD SAVORY SNACKLETS

HONEY SRIRACHA CHICKEN WINGS:
Toss chicken wings in a mixture of sriracha, honey, and a touch of soy sauce. Air fry at 380°F (193°C) for 25 minutes, turning halfway through until crispy. These wings are perfect for a spicy-sweet snack during game night or gatherings.

Directions

1. Blend the oatmeal or oat flakes into a fine powder using a coffee grinder or food processor.
2. In a mixing bowl, combine the oatmeal powder, eggs, milk (or kefir), and a pinch of salt. Stir until the mixture is smooth.
3. Let the mixture rest for 10-15 minutes to thicken slightly.
4. Preheat the air fryer to 180°C (356°F).
5. Grease the silikon with a small amount of coconut oil to prevent sticking.
6. Pour half of the batter into the air fryer basket, spreading it out to form a thin layer.
7. Cook for about 5 minutes, then carefully flip the pancake using a spatula and cook for an additional 2-3 minutes, or until both sides are golden brown and cooked through.
8. Repeat with the remaining batter for the second pancake.

Ensure the batter is not too thick; it should spread easily. Adjust cooking times based on your specific air fryer model. Serve warm with your choice of toppings like honey, fruits, or yogurt for added flavor.

Lavash with Chicken and Vegetable Filling

SERVINGS: 2   COOKING TIME: 25 MIN   CALORIES: 400

Ingredients

- Lavash (Armenian flatbread) 5.6oz (160g)
- Low-fat Milk (1%) – 1/2 cup 100g
- Egg – 2 large
- Cheese – 1 cup (100g), grated
- Cooked chicken breast – 1 cup (160g), finely chopped
- Salt and pepper – to taste
- Tomato – 2 medium, sliced
- Frozen or fresh mixed vegetables (such as peas, broccoli, and carrots) – 1 cup (120g)

ADD SAVORY SNACKLETS

CRISPY TOFU BITES:
Cube firm tofu and toss with soy sauce, cornstarch, and your choice of seasoning like chili powder or garlic powder. Air fry at 400°F (204°C) for about 15 minutes, shaking the basket halfway through, until all sides are crispy. Serve with a dipping sauce like peanut sauce or sweet chili sauce for a delicious vegan treat.

Directions

1. In a mixing bowl, whisk together milk and eggs.

2. Add the grated cheese to the milk and egg mixture and stir to combine.

3. Lay the lavash out flat on a clean surface. Evenly spread the mixture of milk, eggs, and cheese over the lavash.

4. Distribute the cooked, chopped chicken, sliced tomatoes, and mixed vegetables evenly over the lavash.

5. Season with salt and pepper.

6. Carefully roll the lavash like a burrito, ensuring the filling stays inside.

7. Preheat the air fryer to 180°C (350°F).

8. Place the rolled lavash in the air fryer and cook for about 20 minutes or until the exterior is golden and crispy.

9. Halfway through cooking, use tongs to gently turn the lavash roll to ensure even cooking.

10. Once done, remove from the air fryer and let it cool slightly before slicing.

- Ensure that the lavash roll is not too thick to allow for even cooking in the air fryer.

- For a crispy outer layer, you may spray the lavash with a light coating of cooking oil before air frying.

- Adjust cooking time depending on the size and power of your air fryer.

- Serve hot, sliced into portions. Great for a hearty breakfast or a quick dinner!

Oatmeal Shrimp Pizza

SERVINGS: 2   COOKING TIME: 25 MIN   CALORIES: 520

Ingredients

- Oat flakes or oat flour, 2 cups (200 g)
- Kefir/Yogurt (up to 2.5% fat), 1 1/4 cups (300 ml)
- Egg, 2 units
- Sour cream + Tomato paste/ketchup as per taste, 4 tbsp
- Cherry Tomatoes, 2/3 cup (100 g)
- Hard cheese, 1/2 cup (60 g)
- Peeled shrimp, 1 cup (120 g)
- Spices and herbs to taste

ADD SAVORY SNACKLETS

RICOTTA AND SPINACH FILO BITES:
Mix ricotta cheese with finely chopped spinach, a pinch of nutmeg, and some cracked black pepper. Place a spoonful of the mixture on a filo pastry square, fold it over to form a triangle, and brush with a little melted butter. Air fry at 375°F (190°C) for 8-10 minutes until golden and crispy. These elegant bites are great for parties or as a light snack

Directions

1. Blend the oat flakes, eggs, and kefir/yogurt in a processor until smooth.

2. Pour the mixture into a baking dish suitable for the air fryer. Cook at 180°C (350°F) for about 10 minutes.

3. In the meantime, mix sour cream and tomato paste/ketchup in a bowl.

4. When the base is somewhat firm, spread the sour cream and tomato mixture over it.

5. Top with evenly sliced tomatoes, shrimp, and shredded cheese.

6. Cook in the air fryer for an additional 12-15 minutes at the same temperature until the cheese is melted and lightly golden.

7. Garnish with fresh herbs and season with pepper and oregano before serving.

Ensure that the shrimp is properly cleaned and deveined before use. Check the pizza after the first 10 minutes of cooking. For a crispier base, pre-cook the oatmeal mixture slightly longer before adding toppings. Adjust spices according to personal preference.

Lavash with Cheese ("2 Cheese")

SERVINGS: 2   COOKING TIME: 10-12 MIN   CALORIES: 400

Ingredients

- Lavash 2.1 oz (60 g)
- Cottage cheese 1 cup (200 g)
- Parsley or dill 1/4 cup 20 g
- Tomato 2/3 cup (100 g)
- Mozzarella cheese 1/3 cup (40 g)
- Egg 1
- Butter 3 tbsp (50 g)

ADD SAVORY SNACKLETS

PESTO STUFFED MUSHROOMS:
Remove the stems from button mushrooms and fill each cap with a spoonful of store-bought or homemade pesto. Sprinkle with grated mozzarella cheese and air fry at 360°F (182°C) for about 6-8 minutes until the mushrooms are tender and the cheese is bubbly. These make a perfect quick appetizer or a tasty side dish.

Directions

1. Finely chop the tomatoes and parsley or dill.
2. Spread out the lavash flat.
3. Evenly distribute the sour milk cheese over the lavash.
4. Sprinkle the tomato, dill or parsley mixture on top.
5. Grate the mozzarella cheese and scatter it over the tomato layer.
6. Tightly roll the lavash to enclose the filling.
7. Melt the butter and lightly brush it all over the rolled lavash.
8. Preheat the air fryer to 180 degrees Celsius (356 degrees Fahrenheit).
9. Place the rolls in the air fryer basket, ensuring they do not touch each other to allow for even cooking.
10. Air fry for about 7 minutes, then flip and continue to air fry for an additional 3-5 minutes or until golden and crispy.
11. Serve hot, garnished with an optional sprinkle of black cumin seeds on top if desired.

- Adjust cooking times slightly depending on the specific air fryer model and desired crispiness.
- Serve immediately for best texture.
- The calorie count is an estimate and may vary based on specific ingredients used.

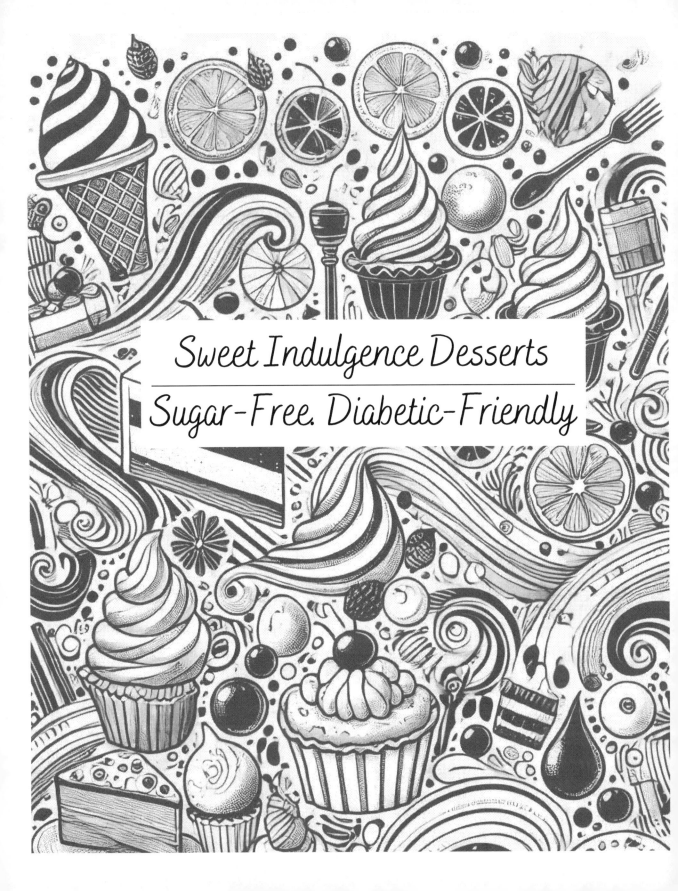

Sweet Indulgence Desserts
Sugar-Free. Diabetic-Friendly

Heaven's Berry Medley Crumble

COOKING TIME: 20 MIN   CALORIES PER PORTION: 200 KCAL   CALORIES/100 GR: 180 KCAL

Ingredients

- 2 cups mixed berries (raspberries, blueberries, strawberries) – 400 grams
- 1/2 cup old-fashioned oats – 50 grams
- 1/4 cup almond flour – 28 grams
- 1/4 cup chopped nuts (almonds, walnuts, pecans) – 28 grams
- 2 tablespoons SweetLeaf Stevia or other sugar substitute – 30 mL
- 1/2 teaspoon cinnamon – 2.5 mL
- 1/4 teaspoon nutmeg – 1.25 mL
- 2 tablespoons melted coconut oil – 30 mL
- 1 tablespoon water – 15 mL

ADD SAVORY SNACKLETS

SESAME GINGER CHICKEN BITES:
Toss diced chicken breasts with soy sauce, sesame oil, minced ginger, and garlic. Coat with sesame seeds and air fry at 390°F (199°C) for about 12 minutes, shaking halfway through. Enjoy these flavorful chicken bites on their own or as part of a meal.

Directions

1. In a mixing bowl, combine berries and water. Set aside.

2. In a separate bowl, stir together oats, almond flour, chopped nuts, SweetLeaf Stevia, cinnamon, and nutmeg.

3. Pour in the melted coconut oil and stir until the mixture forms small clumps.

4. Use a multi-functional air fryer with baking function. Set the temperature to 350°F or 175°C.

5. Put half of the oats mixture in the baking dish, then spread the berries on top.

6. Cover the fruit with the remaining oats mixture.

7. Bake inside the air fryer for 15-20 minutes, until the crumble is golden and the fruit is bubbling.

8. Allow to cool for a few minutes before serving.

This Heaven's Berry Medley Crumble is not just a treat for the tastebuds, but also a boost for your health. Packed with antioxidant-rich berries, heart-healthy oats, and almond flour, this dessert is low in sugar but high in flavor. Plus, it offers a delightful contrast of textures between the juicy berries and crunchy oat crumble topping. What's great about this recipe is that it's forgiving—feel free to mix and match with your favorite berries or nuts. It also makes your kitchen smell fantastic as it bakes in your air fryer. With every bite of this crumble, you're getting a sweet treat and a serving of fruit all in one go! Enjoy this guilt-free delicacy!

Pineapple Paradise with Coconut Shavings

COOKING TIME: 20 MIN   CALORIES PER PORTION: 175 KCAL   CALORIES/100 GR: 158 KCAL

Ingredients

- 1/2 of large Pineapple (cut into 1-inch cubes), approx. 1 cup (240 ml)
- 1 1/2 tbsp of Erythritol or other sugar substitute equivalent (22 ml)
- 1/4 cup of Unsweetened Coconut Flakes (60 ml)
- 1 tsp of Lime Juice (5 ml)
- 1/4 tsp of Ground Cinnamon (1.2 ml)
- Pinch of Salt

ADD SAVORY SNACKLETS

GARLIC PARMESAN BRUSSEL SPROUTS: Halve Brussel sprouts and toss with olive oil, minced garlic, grated Parmesan, salt, and pepper. Air fry at 375°F (190°C) for about 12 minutes, shaking halfway through. Serve these crispy veggies as a healthy side dish or snack.

Directions

1. In a large bowl, combine pineapple cubes and erythritol. Toss until pineapple is nicely coated with the sugar substitute.
2. Spread the sweetened pineapple cubes in the air fryer basket in a single layer, ensuring they do not overlap.
3. Set the air fryer to 375°F (190°C) and cook for 10 minutes.
4. Halfway through the cooking time, give the pineapple a good shake to make sure it cooks evenly.
5. While the pineapple is cooking, spread coconut flakes onto a baking pan. Set the air fryer to 375°F (190°C) and cook the coconut flakes for about 3 minutes, or until they turn golden brown. Keep an eye on them to ensure they don't burn.
6. Once both pineapple and coconut shavings are cooked, toss them together in a large bowl.
7. Drizzle lime juice over the pineapple and coconut mix.
8. Sprinkle with ground cinnamon and a pinch of salt.
9. Mix well and serve warm for the best flavor.

This tropical dessert is not only visually appealing with its vibrant, sunny color but also packs a nutritious punch. Pineapple is a great source of vitamin C for immune health and bromelain, a natural enzyme that promotes digestion. The coconut shavings add a satisfying crunch, alongside healthy fats and fiber. This dish is a wonderful way to satisfy your sweet tooth while keeping your sugar intake at bay, making it a diabetic-friendly indulgence. Remember, the best part of any dessert is sharing it with someone you cherish, so don't forget to make enough for two!

Apple Cinnamon Muffins

COOKING TIME: 20 MIN   CALORIES PER PORTION: 80 KCAL   CALORIES/100 GR: 106 KCAL

Ingredients

- 1 cup of whole wheat flour (120g)
- 1/2 cup of zero-calorie natural sweetener (96g)
- 1 teaspoon of baking powder (4g)
- 1/2 teaspoon of baking soda (2g)
- 1/2 teaspoon of ground cinnamon (1g)
- 1 medium-sized apple, cored and chop into small pieces (about 1 cup or 120g)
- 1 large egg (50g),
- 1/2 cup of unsweetened almond milk (120g)
- 2 tablespoons of unsweetened applesauce (30g)

ADD SAVORY SNACKLETS

BANANA CHIPS:
Slice bananas thinly, sprinkle with a little cinnamon and sugar, and air fry at 350°F (177°C) for about 10 minutes until crisp. These banana chips are a healthy alternative to store-bought snacks and perfect for on-the-go munching.

Directions

1. Mix whole wheat flour, natural sweetener, baking powder, baking soda, and cinnamon in a mixing bowl.
2. In a separate bowl, whisk together the chopped apple, egg, almond milk, and applesauce.
3. Gradually add the dry ingredient mixture into the wet ingredients, stirring until fully combined.
4. Divide the batter evenly among six silicone muffin cups.
5. Arrange the muffin cups in the air fryer basket.
6. Cook at 320°F (160°C) for 12 minutes, or until a toothpick inserted into a muffin comes out clean.
7. Allow the muffins to cool for some minutes before handling.

These mouthwatering apple cinnamon muffins are packed with fiber and refreshingly sweet apple bits. Whole wheat flour gives you a dose of grains, and using zero-calorie natural sweetener keeps this dessert diabetic-friendly. The aromatic cinnamon isn't just for adding flavor, it also has anti-inflammatory properties which improve your heart health. All these benefits while pleasing your sweet tooth. Aren't air fryers fantastic?

Berry Delight Air Fryer Pavlovas

COOKING TIME: 20 MIN   CALORIES PER PORTION: 135 KCAL   CALORIES/100 GR: 90 KCAL

Ingredients

- 5 large egg whites (Room temperature)
- 1 cup of granulated Stevia (210 grams)
- 1 teaspoon vanilla extract (5 grams)
- 1 teaspoon white vinegar (5 grams)
- 1 tablespoon cornstarch (8 grams)
- 1/2 cup heavy whipping cream (118 ml)
- 2 cups mixed fresh berries (such as strawberries, raspberries, and blueberries) (300 grams)

ADD SAVORY SNACKLETS

SPICY CAULIFLOWER POPCORN:
Cut cauliflower into small florets and coat with olive oil, paprika, and chili powder. Air fry at 380°F (193°C) for 10-12 minutes, shaking halfway through until crispy. These make a fantastic spicy snack or a great addition to a salad

Directions

1. Start by separating your egg whites, ensuring no yolk contamination, as this can prevent your whites from whipping as needed.

2. In a clean and dry mixing bowl, beat the egg whites on low speed until soft peaks form.

3. Gradually, while continuing to beat the egg whites, add the granulated Stevia and increase the speed to medium. Add in the vanilla extract, white vinegar, and cornstarch and beat until stiff peaks form.

4. Form four even-sized mounds of egg-white mixture on the air fryer basket, leaving space in between each mound.

5. Cook at 250°F (120°C) for 15 minutes without opening the air fryer. After the time has elapsed, allow the pavlovas to sit in the air fryer for another 5 minutes to continue to set.

6. While the pavlovas are cooling, whip the heavy cream in a chilled bowl until soft peaks form.

7. After the pavlovas have completely cooled, spoon the whipped cream on top and garnish with the mixed berries. Serve and enjoy!

Pavlovas are a delightful dessert option that align well with a diabetic-friendly diet, due to the use of Stevia as a sugar substitute. The berries provide a handful of great antioxidants, while the whipped cream offers an indulgent touch to this low-calorie dessert. Remember, while the pavlovas are air frying, resist the temptation to peek! The cooking process depends on steady heat, so frequent opening of the air fryer will lead to a less than perfect dessert. Enjoy the light sweetness and matchless texture of these delightful pavlovas, perfect for a couple's dessert night!

Cinnamon Apple Crumble

COOKING TIME: 20 MIN   CALORIES PER PORTION: 230 KCAL   CALORIES/100 GR: 390 KCAL

Ingredients

- 2 Apples, medium-sized
(Peeled, cored and thinly sliced)
- 2 tbsp Granulated Erythritol (30 grams)
- 1 tsp Ground Cinnamon (5 grams)
- 1/2 cup Old-Fashioned Rolled Oats
(120 grams)
- 2 tbsp Coconut Oil (Melted) (30 grams)
- A pinch of Salt

Directions

1. In a large mixing bowl, toss the apple slices with Erythritol and half of the cinnamon until well coated.

2. Layer the seasoned apples on the bottom of the air fryer dish.

3. In the same bowl, combine rolled oats, the rest of the cinnamon, coconut oil, and a pinch of salt. Stir until the oats are well coated.

4. Sprinkle the oat mixture over the apples, creating a crumble-like texture.

5. Cook in the air fryer at 350F/180C for 10-15 minutes or until the top is browned and the apples are tender.

6. Allow to cool for a couple of minutes before serving.

ADD TASTY BITES

CHICKEN PARMESAN MEATBALLS:
Combine ground chicken, grated Parmesan, breadcrumbs, and Italian seasoning. Form into balls and air fry at 390°F (199°C) for 10 minutes or until cooked through. Serve with pasta and marinara sauce for a quick meal.

This Cinnamon Apple Air Fryer Crumble is a sweet indulgence without the guilt. Cinnamon's warm flavors perfectly contrast with the tartness of the apples while the oat topping adds a wholesome crunch. Erythritol is used as a sugar substitute, making it an excellent choice for those keeping an eye on their sugar intake. Plus, oats are high in fiber, aiding digestion and leaving you feeling satisfied without overloading on calories. So sit back, relax, and enjoy this sweet treat that won't derail your diet!

Orange Muffins

COOKING TIME: 25 MIN   CALORIES PER PORTION: 160   CALORIES/100 GR: 230 KCAL

Ingredients

- Orange - 6-10 units (10 if small), tangerines can also be used
- Eggs - 5 units
- 1 1/2 cups Oat flour
- Baking powder - 2 teaspoons
- Yogurt - 4 teaspoons
- Stevia - 4 teaspoons
- Orange juice - 140 ml

ADD SAVORY SNACKLETS

HERBED POTATO WEDGES:
Cut potatoes into wedges and toss with olive oil, rosemary, thyme, salt, and pepper. Air fry at 400°F (204°C) for about 15-20 minutes. Serve these crispy wedges with a side of sour cream or ketchup.

Directions

1. Cut the tops off the oranges and remove the pulp carefully using a knife or spoon.

2. Blend the orange pulp using a blender or food processor.

3. In a bowl, mix the eggs, yogurt, stevia, baking powder, oat flour, and rolled oats together until well combined.

4. Add the blended orange pulp and 140 ml of orange juice to the bowl and mix to create a batter.

5. Carefully spoon the batter back into the hollowed-out orange peels, filling them just below the top edge to allow space for the batter to rise.

6. Place the filled orange cups in the air fryer basket, ensuring they are stable and won't tip over.

7. Cook in the air fryer at 180°C (356°F) for about 20-25 minutes or until the muffins are firm and a toothpick inserted into the center comes out clean.

- Ensure the orange cups are stable in the air fryer to prevent them from tipping over during cooking.
- You can use muffin liners or small ramekins if the orange shells are not stable enough.
- The sweet level can be adjusted by increasing or decreasing the amount of Stevia according to taste.
- Serve warm for best taste and texture

Raspberry Almond Squares

COOKING TIME: 20 MIN   CALORIES PER PORTION: 235 KCAL   CALORIES/100 GR: 265 KCAL

Ingredients

- 1 cup almond flour (120 g)
- ½ cup of a sugar substitute like Erythritol (100 g)
- 1 large egg
- 1 tsp vanilla extract (5 ml)
- 1/2 cup fresh raspberries (61.5 g)
- 2 tbsp sliced almonds (18 g)
- Pinch of salt

Directions

1. In a medium mixing bowl, combine the almond flour, erythritol, and pinch of salt.
2. Crack open the egg and add it to the same bowl alongside the vanilla extract. Stir everything well until a firm dough forms.
3. Flatten the dough on an air fryer safe pan that fits inside your air fryer.
4. Gently press the fresh raspberries into the dough and sprinkle the sliced almonds on top.
5. Place the pan in the air fryer compatible rack.
6. Set the air fryer at 320°F (160°C) and cook for 12 15 minutes or until the edges are golden brown.
7. Take out the pan carefully (it will be hot), let it cool and cut the pastry into squares.

ADD TASTY BITES

BACON-WRAPPED DATES:
Wrap pitted dates with half-slices of bacon and secure with toothpicks. Air fry at 390°F (200°C) for 10 minutes or until the bacon is crispy. These sweet and savory bites are perfect for a quick appetizer or snack.

These Raspberry Almond Squares are 100% sugar-free and yet delightfully sweet. This recipe flaunts the mighty almond in three different ways: almond flour as a base, almond extract for that extra kick of flavor, and sliced almonds for a stunningly crunchy top. Raspberries add a fruity tang and beautiful color contrast, making this dessert a real feast for the eye as well as the palate. These squares are not only diabetic-friendly but also gluten-free, which makes them a wonderful dessert option for diverse dietary needs. Enjoy them as a guilt-free treat after dinner or a mid-afternoon snack. Just remember to keep your portions in check!

Apple Cinnamon Delight Cups

COOKING TIME: 20 MIN   CALORIES PER PORTION: 190 KCAL   CALORIES/100 GR: 240 KCAL

Ingredients

- 2 medium apples, peeled and cored (approx. 180g)
- 1 teaspoon ground cinnamon (approx. 5g)
- 1 tablespoon granulated sweetener, sugar-free (approx. 14g)
- A pinch of salt
- Non-stick cooking spray
- 1 cup almond flour (approx. 100g)
- 1/2 tablespoon unsalted butter, melted (approx. 8g)
- 1/2 teaspoon vanilla extract (approx. 2g)

ADD SAVORY SNACKLETS

ASPARAGUS AND PROSCIUTTO WRAPS:
Wrap thin slices of prosciutto around asparagus spears. Lightly brush with olive oil and season with black pepper. Air fry at 400°F (200°C) for 7-9 minutes until the asparagus is tender and the prosciutto is crispy. This dish serves as a fancy yet easy appetizer or side.

Directions

1. Chop the peeled and cored apples into small pieces.

2. In a bowl, mix the chopped apples, ground cinnamon, granulated sugar-free sweetener, and a pinch of salt.

3. In a separate bowl, combine the almond flour, melted unsalted butter, and vanilla extract. This will form the base of our delight cups.

4. Spray the air fryer basket with the non-stick cooking spray.

5. Divide the almond flour mixture into two parts. Press each part into the bottom of two air fryer safe containers.

6. Divide the apple mixture into two portions and spread it over the almond flour base in each container.

7. Place the containers in the air fryer basket, ensuring enough space is left around them for air to circulate.

8. Cook at 325°F (165°C) for 15 minutes, or until the apples are soft and cooked through.

9. Let it cool for a few minutes and your Apple Cinnamon Delight Cups are ready to serve!

These Apple Cinnamon Delight Cups are a perfect dessert for health-conscious individuals. With a base of almond flour and sugar-free sweetener, they're low-carb and perfectly suited for those managing diabetes or following a keto diet. The sweet, spiced apple topping gives a comforting flavor that's hard to resist. Plus, who can say no to the wonderful aroma of cinnamon and apples mingling together? As an added bonus, apples are a great source of vitamins and fiber. Now you can enjoy dessert without any guilt, isn't that delightful?

Tropical Coconut & Mango Custard Cups

COOKING TIME: 20 MIN   CALORIES PER PORTION: 225 KCAL   CALORIES/100 GR: 115 KCAL

Ingredients

- 1 large ripe Mango
(peeled and diced into small pieces)
- 2 large Eggs
- 1 cup of Organic Coconut Milk (240 ml)
- 1/2 cup of Granulated Erythritol (120 g)
- 1/2 teaspoon of pure Vanilla Extract
(2 ml)
- Shredded Coconut for garnishing

ADD SAVORY SNACKLETS

MINI VEGGIE QUICHE CUPS:
Whisk together eggs, milk, chopped onions, bell peppers, spinach, and cheese. Pour into silicone muffin cups and place in the air fryer. Cook at 360°F (182°C) for about 8-10 minutes or until the eggs are set. These mini quiches are perfect for breakfast on the go or a healthy snack.

Directions

1. Combine eggs, coconut milk, erythritol, and vanilla extract in a large bowl. Whisk until all ingredients are well incorporated.

2. Distribute the diced mango equally into two heatproof ramekins or small bowls.

3. Pour the egg and coconut milk mixture over the mango in the ramekins, ensuring the fruit is fully submerged.

4. Place the ramekins in the air fryer basket, making sure they do not touch each other.

5. Set the air fryer at 320°F (160°C) and cook for 15 minutes.

6. After the custard has set, using the air fryer's tongs, carefully remove the ramekins and allow them to cool.

7. Once cooled, garnish with shredded coconut and serve.

This tropical treat celebrates the exotic flavors of coconut and mango, which are not only delicious but also highly beneficial for your health. Mangoes are known for their high levels of vitamins C and A, while coconuts provide healthy fats and are high in fiber. These custard cups are not only delightful desserts but also a sweet way to make a balanced diet more enjoyable. We have used Erythritol, a sugar alcohol, as our choice of sweetener which has virtually no calories and does not affect blood sugar or insulin levels, making it an excellent choice for diabetics. Enjoy this sweet indulgence guilt-free!

Chocolate Raspberry Air-Fried Cheesecake Cups

COOKING TIME: 20 MIN   CALORIES PER PORTION: 195 KCAL   CALORIES/100 GR: 244 KCAL

Ingredients

- 8 Ounces Cream Cheese (230 grams)
- 2 Large Eggs
- 1/2 Cup Stevia Sweetener (120 grams)
- 1 Teaspoon Vanilla Extract (5 ml)
- 2 Tablespoons Almond Flour (30 grams)
- 1/2 Cup Raspberries (65 grams)
- 1/2 Cup Dark Chocolate Chips - Sugar-Free (90 grams)

ADD TASTY BITES

HONEY GLAZED SALMON BITES:
Cut salmon into bite-sized pieces and marinate in a mixture of honey, soy sauce, and minced garlic. Thread the salmon pieces onto skewers and air fry at 400°F (204°C) for 5-7 minutes, turning once. These bites offer a deliciously sweet and savory flavor, ideal for a quick dinner or appetizer.

Directions

1. Start by blending the cream cheese, eggs, stevia, vanilla extract, and almond flour in a food processor until smooth.

2. Once your mix is ready, prepare your air fryer safe muffin cups by lining them with parchment paper.

3. Pour the blended mixture into each pudding cup, filling them to about half.

4. Next, sprinkle a few raspberries and chocolate chips evenly over each cup.

5. Arrange the muffin cups in the air fryer basket, ensuring that they don't touch each other or the sides of the basket.

6. Set the temperature to 300°F or 150 °C, and cook for 15 minutes.

7. After 15 minutes, insert a toothpick into the center of the cheesecake. If it comes out clean, your cheesecake is ready. If not, cook for another 2-3 minutes and check again.

8. Once they are cooked, remove them from the air fryer and let cool before serving.

Enjoy these delightfully decadent yet health-conscious Chocolate Raspberry Air-Fried Cheesecake Cups. They're sugar-free, making them a wonderful dessert option suitable for those living with diabetes or anyone following a low-sugar diet. The almond flour and dark chocolate chips provide healthy fats, fiber, and protein, while the raspberries add a refreshing burst of fruity goodness. Plus, cooking in an air fryer means we're maintaining all the creaminess of a traditional cheesecake, but making it lighter and quicker. These are perfect to be served at your next small gathering or simply as an after-dinner treat.

Cinnamon Apple Crisp

COOKING TIME: 20 MIN   CALORIES PER PORTION: 124 KCAL   CALORIES/100 GR: 115 KCAL

Ingredients

- 2 medium-sized apples (343 grams)
- 1/4 cup of old-fashioned oats (19.75 grams)
- 2 tablespoons of almond flour (14 grams)
- 1 tablespoon of melted coconut oil (16 grams)
- 1 tablespoon of cinnamon (7.8 grams)
- 2 tablespoons of sugar-free maple syrup (30 grams)
- A pinch of salt (0.5 grams)

ADD SAVORY SNACKLETS

SWEET AND SPICY NUT MIX:
Toss a combination of your favorite nuts with maple syrup, cinnamon, cayenne pepper, and a pinch of salt. Air fry at 340°F (171°C) for 6-7 minutes, stirring occasionally, until golden and fragrant. This nut mix is a fantastic snack for a flavorful energy boost.

Directions

1. Start by coring your apples and cutting them into thin slices. You can leave the peels on for added nutrients.

2. In a medium-sized bowl, combine the oats, almond flour, melted coconut oil, cinnamon, sugar-free maple syrup, and a pinch of salt.

3. Toss the apple slices in the mixture until they're fully coated.

4. Make sure the apple slices are evenly distributed in the air fryer's basket. Cook them at 350°F (175°C) for 10 minutes.

5. After 10 minutes, gently stir the apples using a silicone spatula for even cooking. Continue to cook for another 5-7 minutes or until the apples are tender and the oat mixture becomes crispy.

6. Allow it to cool for a few minutes before serving.

This delicious Cinnamon Apple Crisp recipe is not only sugar-free and diabetic-friendly but it's packed with dietary fibers, healthy fats, and antioxidants from the cinnamon and apples. The air fryer achieves a perfect balance of tenderness and crispiness, making this dessert as tasty as it is guilt-free. You can serve this delicious dessert with a scoop of sugar-free ice cream for an extra-indulgent treat. Just remember to count those calories! No minute will be wasted in making this healthy, quick, and delightful dessert!

Chocolate Almond Air Fryer Brownies

COOKING TIME: 20 MIN   CALORIES PER PORTION: 270 KCAL   CALORIES/100 GR: 415 KCAL

Ingredients

- 1/2 cup (113 g) unsalted butter
- 1/2 cup (120 ml) honey
- 1/2 cup (43 g) unsweetened cocoa powder
- 2 large eggs
- 1 teaspoon (5 ml) vanilla extract
- 1/3 cup (40 g) almond meal/almond flour
- 1/4 teaspoon salt
- 1/2 cup (75 g) sugar-free dark chocolate chips
- 1/4 cup (35 g) chopped almonds

ADD TASTY BITES

GARLIC LEMON SHRIMP SKEWERS:
Thread peeled shrimp onto skewers and season with olive oil, minced garlic, lemon zest, salt, and pepper. Air fry at 400°F (204°C) for 6-8 minutes, flipping halfway through, until shrimp are pink and cooked through. These skewers are bursting with flavor and make a great light entrée or appetizer.

Directions

1. In a microwave-safe bowl, melt the butter.
2. Stir in the honey until well combined, then mix in the cocoa powder.
3. Once this mixture has cooled slightly, add in the eggs and vanilla extract. Stir until smooth.
4. Add the almond meal and salt, mixing until everything is well combined.
5. Fold in the chocolate chips and chopped almonds.
6. Divide this mixture into silicone muffin cups or a greased air fryer pan, filling only about 2/3 of the way full.
7. Insert the pan or muffin cups into the air fryer. Set the air fryer to 320°F (160°C) for 10-12 minutes or until a toothpick inserted into the center comes out clean.
8. Allow the brownies to cool before serving!

Slip into sweet indulgence with these Chocolate Almond Air Fryer Brownies. With no processed sugar and rich in antioxidants from the dark chocolate, this treat pleases your sweet tooth without piling on the guilt. It's also gluten-free, thanks to the almond meal, and packed with healthy fats. Remember, a healthy diet means balance, and yes – that can include chocolate! A perfect partner for your Netflix binge nights or when you're craving a quick, gooey dessert. Remember: moderation is key! Happy eating!

Decadent Cacao-Berry Muffins

COOKING TIME: 20 MIN   CALORIES PER PORTION: 243 KCAL   CALORIES/100 GR: 252 KCAL

Ingredients

- 1/2 cup (120 grams) packed almond flour
- 2 tablespoons (about 28 grams) cacao powder
- 1/8 teaspoon (about 0.6 grams) stevia
- 1/2 teaspoon (about 2.5 grams) baking powder
- 2 large eggs
- 1/4 cup (about 60ml) unsweetened almond milk
- 1/2 cup (about 75 grams) fresh or frozen mixed berries

ADD SAVORY SNACKLETS

PARMESAN TOMATO BITES:
Slice roma tomatoes into halves, top each with a mixture of breadcrumbs, shredded Parmesan cheese, Italian seasoning, and a drizzle of olive oil. Air fry at 390°F (199°C) for about 5-7 minutes until the topping is golden and crispy. These bites are perfect for a flavorful snack.

Directions

1. In a microwave-safe bowl, melt the butter.
2. Stir in the honey until well combined, then mix in the cocoa powder.
3. Once this mixture has cooled slightly, add in the eggs and vanilla extract. Stir until smooth.
4. Add the almond meal and salt, mixing until everything is well combined.
5. Fold in the chocolate chips and chopped almonds.
6. Divide this mixture into silicone muffin cups or a greased air fryer pan, filling only about 2/3 of the way full.
7. Insert the pan or muffin cups into the air fryer. Set the air fryer to 320°F (160°C) for 10-12 minutes or until a toothpick inserted into the center comes out clean.
8. Allow the brownies to cool before serving!

These Decadent Cacao-Berry Muffins are not only delicious and indulgent but also fall well within the realms of healthy eating. Cacao is a great source of antioxidants, and using almond flour instead of regular flour lowers the carbohydrate content and adds a generous amount of protein. Stevia, a natural sweetener, brings the sweet flavor to these muffins without adding any unwanted sugars, perfect for those who are watching their sugar intake or managing diabetes. The incorporation of mixed berries provides a burst of freshness and a boost of fiber. With these muffins, you'll satisfy your sweet tooth while keeping your health in check! Enjoy a dessert that loves you back.

Berry Bliss Air Fryer Meringues

COOKING TIME: 27 MIN   CALORIES PER PORTION: 50 KCAL   CALORIES/100 GR: 40 KCAL

Ingredients

- 1/2 Cup Egg Whites (approximately 4 large eggs) (118 ml)
- 1/2 Teaspoon Cream of Tartar (2.5 ml)
- 1 Cup Stevia (200 grams)
- 1 Cup Mixed Berries (200 grams)
- 1 Teaspoon Vanilla Extract (5 ml)
- 1 Pinch Sea Salt

ADD SAVORY SNACKLETS

COCONUT BANANA BITES:
Slice bananas into coins, dip in a light batter of flour and coconut milk, then roll in shredded coconut. Air fry at 350°F (177°C) for 8-10 minutes until golden and crispy. These tropical treats are excellent as a dessert or a sweet afternoon snack.

Directions

1. In a clean, dry bowl, whip the egg whites with a pinch of sea salt until they form soft peaks. This should take approximately 5 minutes.

2. Gradually add in the cream of tartar and stevia while continuing to whip the mixture. Whisk until it forms stiff peaks.

3. Fold in the mixed berries and vanilla extract gently to avoid deflating the egg whites.

4. Spoon the meringue mixture onto a parchment-lined air fryer tray, making sure to leave room between each for them to expand.

5. Using the baking function, set your air fryer to 310°F and bake for 10 minutes. After 10 minutes, reduce the heat to 200°F and bake for another 8 minutes.

6. Let the meringues cool for 2 minutes before carefully removing them.

As well as being a delight to the taste buds, these Berry Bliss Air Fryer Meringues are naturally low in calories and contain no refined sugar, making them a healthier choice for dessert lovers. The mixed berries present in these meringues are packed full of essential vitamins, fiber and antioxidants that can contribute to overall health. The air fryer's circulating heat cooks the meringues evenly, giving them a light and crisp texture that's hard to resist. You'll love the surprise burst of sweetness from the mixed berries in every bite!

Did You Know? Meringues were invented in Switzerland, and are traditionally baked in a slow oven for several hours. Thanks to the air fryer, you can now have these sweet treats ready in just 20 minutes!

Raspberry Bliss Bars

COOKING TIME: 27 MIN   CALORIES PER PORTION: 390 KCAL   CALORIES/100 GR: 400 KCAL

Ingredients

- 1 Cup of Ground Almonds (90g)
- 1/4 Cup Cocoa Powder (25g)
- 2 Tablespoons of Honey (60ml)
- 4 Tablespoons of Coconut Oil (60ml)
- 1 Cup of Fresh Raspberries (110g)
- 3 Tablespoons of Chia Seeds (45ml)

ADD SAVORY SNACKLETS

ROSEMARY ROASTED CASHEWS:
Toss cashews with olive oil, fresh rosemary, salt, and a sprinkle of brown sugar. Air fry at 340°F (171°C) for about 8 minutes, shaking the basket occasionally, until golden and fragrant. Enjoy as a savory snack that's perfect for gatherings or quiet evenings at home.

Directions

1. Begin by gathering all of your ingredients to ensure you have everything at hand. This can make the process quicker and simpler.

2. Prepare the crust by combining the ground almonds and the cocoa powder in a mixing bowl.

3. Melt the coconut oil and honey in the microwave, then mix these wet ingredients into the almond-cocoa mix until well combined.

4. Firmly press this mixture into the air fryer-safe pan, creating an even layer of crust.

5. In a separate bowl, mash the raspberries and chia seeds together until they form a nice puree.

6. Pour the raspberry-chia mix over the prepared crust, spreading evenly.

7. Pop the pan into your air fryer, adjust the temperature to 350°F (180°C) and set the timer for 15 minutes.

8. After the timer beeps, carefully remove the pan from the air fryer and let it cool before refrigerating for an hour.

These Raspberry Bliss Bars are not just delicious - they're a truly healthy dessert choice. The ingredients are all natural and low in sugar. Raspberries and chia seeds make a fantastic combination, providing a burst of antioxidants, fiber and omega-3 fatty acids. Additionally, the almond-cocoa crust gives you a dose of healthy fats and reduces the overall number of carbs. Enjoy this dessert with a light heart, knowing that you are treating yourself and keeping your health in mind.

Luscious Lemon Blueberry Shortcakes

COOKING TIME: 23 MIN   CALORIES PER PORTION: 200 KCAL   CALORIES/100 GR: 269 KCAL

Ingredients

1 cup almond flour (120 grams)

1/4 cup coconut flour (30 grams)

1 tsp baking powder (5 grams)

1/4 tsp salt (1 gram)

Zest and juice of 1 lemon

3 large eggs

2 tbsp coconut oil, melted (30 ml)

1 tsp vanilla extract (5 ml)

2 tbsp Erythritol or other sugar substitute (30 grams)

1 cup blueberries, fresh or frozen (150 grams)

For topping:

½ cup heavy cream, whipped (60 ml)

A handful of fresh blueberries

ADD TASTY BITES

GARLIC AND PARMESAN GREEN BEAN FRIES:
Trim fresh green beans and toss with olive oil, minced garlic, grated Parmesan, salt, and pepper. Air fry at 400°F (204°C) for 10-12 minutes, shaking halfway through, until crispy. These make a fantastic side dish or a healthy snack alternative.

Directions

1. In a medium bowl, mix the almond flour, coconut flour, baking powder, salt, and lemon zest.

2. In another bowl, beat the eggs together with the lemon juice, melted coconut oil, vanilla extract, and sweetener of choice.

3. Gradually mix the dry ingredients into the wet ones until you have a consistent batter.

4. Gently fold in the blueberries.

5. Divide the batter into six portions and form each into a disk shape.

6. Place the disks in the basket of the air fryer, making sure they don't touch.

7. Set the air fryer to 320F (160C) and bake for 10-12 minutes, or until the shortcakes are golden brown.

8. Once done, let them cool for a few minutes.

9. Slice each shortcake in half and fill with whipped cream and a few fresh blueberries. Serve immediately.

These wonderful Lemon Blueberry Shortcakes are easy to make with your air fryer and are perfect for a quick dessert. They're packed full of natural flavors, being both zesty from the lemon and sweet from the blueberries. As they use almond and coconut flour, this recipe is gluten-free and perfect for those following a keto or low-carb diet. They also take advantage of the air fryer's ability to bake desserts without heating up the whole kitchen, thus saving energy, time, and effort. The dreamy cream paired with fresh blueberries and moist cake layers create an elegant dessert that tantalizes your taste buds. Indulge in this delightful dessert without any guilt!

Carob-Cherry Delight Bites

COOKING TIME: 23 MIN   CALORIES PER PORTION: 250 KCAL   CALORIES/100 GR: 210 KCAL

Ingredients

- 1 cup of carob chips (175 grams)
- 1/2 cup of almond flour (50 grams)
- 1/4 cup of pitted cherries (37.5 grams)
- 1/4 cup of unsweetened applesauce (60 grams)
- 1/2 cup of almond milk (120 ml)
- 2 tablespoons of Stevia (30 grams)
- A pinch of salt

ADD SAVORY SNACKLETS

MOZZARELLA ARANCINI BALLS:
Mix leftover risotto with chopped mozzarella cheese. Form into balls, dip in beaten egg, then roll in breadcrumbs. Air fry at 350°F (177°C) for about 10 minutes, turning once, until they are golden and crispy. These are great served with marinara sauce for dipping.

Directions

1. In a medium mixing bowl, combine the almond flour, carob chips, and a pinch of salt.
2. In a different bowl, blend the pitted cherries, unsweetened applesauce, and stevia.
3. Combine the cherry mixture with the almond flour and carob mixture. Stir until a consistent dough forms.
4. Scoop one tablespoon of the dough, make a ball and place it inside the air fryer basket. Repeat this step until all dough is used up.
5. Set the air fryer at 350F (175C) for 10 minutes. Check occasionally to avoid overcooking.
6. Once done, remove from the air fryer and let cool for a few minutes.
7. Drizzle with almond milk before serving for a bit of extra indulgence.

This delicious dish is a perfect blend of fruity, nutty, and chocolatey flavors packed into a sugar-free bite-sized dessert. The carob chips provide a similar taste to chocolate but are caffeine-free and lower in fat, making them an excellent choice for a light yet satisfying dessert. The use of Stevia as a sweetener instead of sugar makes this recipe diabetic-friendly, and the addition of cherries not only provides a tart contrast but also loads the dish with antioxidants. Not to forget, these delights are dairy-free too, owing to the almond milk drizzling. Enjoy this guilt-free dessert that aligns with your healthy lifestyle and satisfies your sweet tooth!

Delectable Carob Banana Mini Cakes

COOKING TIME: 25 MIN   CALORIES PER PORTION: 138 KCAL   CALORIES/100 GR: 163 KCAL

Ingredients

- 2 ripe Bananas, mashed(200g)
- 1 cup Carob Powder (80g)
- 2 Eggs
- 1 cup Almond Flour (95g)
- 0.5 cup Unsweetened Almond Milk (120ml)
- 1 teaspoon Pure Vanilla Extract (5ml)
- 1 teaspoon Baking Powder (5g)
- 1/3 cup Erythritol, granulated (70g)
- Optional: A pinch of sea salt

ADD SAVORY SNACKLETS

MINI BRIE AND APPLE GRILLED CHEESE: Assemble mini sandwiches with thin slices of apple and brie cheese between small pieces of sourdough bread. Brush the outside with melted butter and air fry at 360°F (182°C) for about 6-8 minutes, flipping halfway through, until golden brown and melty.

Directions

1. In a bowl, combine the mashed bananas, eggs, almond milk, and vanilla extract.

2. In a separate bowl, mix the almond flour, carob powder, baking powder, and erythritol.

3. Combine the wet and dry ingredients and mix until you get a smooth batter.

4. Pour the batter into the silicon muffin cups till halfway, to allow space for them to rise.

5. Place the silicon muffin cups into the air fryer.

6. Set the temperature to 320°F (160°C) and timer to 10 minutes.

7. After 10 minutes, check on the mini cakes, if a toothpick comes out clean when poked, they're done. If not, extend the time to 5 more minutes.

8. Once done, switch off the air fryer and let the cakes cool.

Enjoy these gluten-free and diabetic-friendly carob banana mini cakes guilt-free. Carob powder is a naturally sweet, unusually nutritious substitute to cocoa, rich in fiber and antioxidants, making these mini cakes a perfect healthier dessert option. Almond flour offers a high protein profile and low carbohydrate content, which supports a healthy diet. Erythritol is a sugar-alcohol sweetener, non-nutritive, that does not raise blood glucose or insulin levels. So sit back, relax, and let the air fryer do the magic, delivering a scrumptious, healthy dessert in just 20 minutes. Who said health and taste can't go hand-in-hand?

Air Fryer Carob Powder-Dusted Almond Cookies

COOKING TIME: 25 MIN   CALORIES PER PORTION: 95 KCAL   CALORIES/100 GR: 245 KCAL

Ingredients

- 1 cup Almond flour (100g)
- 1/2 cup Erythritol (100g)
- 2 Eggs
- 1/2 tsp Baking powder (2.5g)
- 1 tsp Vanilla extract (5ml)
- 1 pinch Salt
- 2 tbsp Carob powder (14g), to dust

ADD SAVORY SNACKLETS

RATATOUILLE BITES:
Layer thinly sliced zucchini, yellow squash, eggplant, and tomato with a sprinkle of herbs de Provence in mini tart shells. Air fry at 375°F (190°C) for about 10 minutes until the vegetables are tender and the crust is crisp.

Directions

1. In a large mixing bowl, combine almond flour, Erythritol, baking powder, and salt.

2. Beat the eggs in another bowl and add vanilla extract.

3. Gradually add the mixture of eggs and vanilla extract to the dry ingredients. Stir until you form a homogenous dough.

4. Using a cookie scoop or your hands, shape small cookies and place them into the air fryer basket. Ensure that the cookies are not touching each other.

5. Set your air fryer to 320°F (160°C) and bake for 15 minutes or until the tops of the cookies are firm.

6. Allow the cookies to cool before dusting them with the carob powder.

7. Serve and enjoy!

The Carob Powder-Dusted Almond Cookies not only have a rich and slightly nutty taste, but are also a healthier alternative to regular sugar-laden desserts. Carob powder, in addition to having a lot less fat and calories than chocolate, contains plenty of fiber, calcium, and beneficial antioxidants. Erythritol - a sugar alcohol - is a fantastic healthy substitute for sugar as it contains 0 calories. It does not spike your blood sugar or insulin levels making this recipe perfectly suited to be part of a diabetic-friendly diet. Moreover, the use of almond flour instead of traditional wheat-based flours means these delightful cookies are a source of protein and good fats, low in carbs, and gluten free. Served with a cup of herbal tea, these cookies can satisfy your sweet tooth without making you feel guilty! These mouth-watering treats can be prepared in just 20 minutes using your air fryer - a baking innovation that brings crispy perfection to your desserts while staying on the healthier side. Enjoy this ingenious blend of taste and health!

Carob Delight Bites

COOKING TIME: 25 MIN   CALORIES PER PORTION: 182 KCAL   CALORIES/100 GR: 405 KCAL

Ingredients

- 1 cup almond flour (120 grams)
- ½ cup of carob powder (60 grams)
- 1 tsp baking powder (5 grams)
- ¼ cup of coconut oil, melted (60 ml)
- ¼ cup of sugar-free maple syrup (60 ml)
- 1 egg, large
- 1 tsp pure vanilla extract (5 ml)

ADD SAVORY SNACKLETS

GARLIC AND ROSEMARY POTATO SLICES: Thinly slice potatoes, toss with olive oil, minced garlic, rosemary, salt, and pepper. Air fry at 380°F (193°C) for about 15 minutes, stirring occasionally, until crispy and golden. These make a fragrant and tasty side dish or snack.

Directions

1. In a large bowl, mix together the almond flour, carob powder, and baking powder.

2. In another bowl, whisk together coconut oil, sugar-free maple syrup, egg, and vanilla extract.

3. Pour the liquid mixture into the dry mixture and mix until combined. You should have a stiff dough.

4. Portion the dough by 1 tablespoon and roll into balls. Place the balls in the air fryer basket, making sure they have room to expand.

5. Cook at 350°F (175°C) for 10 minutes, or until they develop a nice crust and no longer look doughy in the center.

6. Let the Carob Delight Bites cool for a few minutes before indulging.

Carob is a healthier alternative to chocolate that offers a similar flavor but boasts less fat and no caffeine. This makes our carob delight bites even more desirable for those who are after a guilt-free treat that caters to their sweet tooth. The heart-healthy fats in the almond flour and coconut oil will keep you feeling satisfied without the sugar crash. Also, these bites are diabetic-friendly; we've utilized sugar-free maple syrup for its natural sweetness and sugar-alternative benefits. So why not whip these up in the air fryer for a quick, easy dessert! They make a delightful end to the day or even as an energy-packed snack anytime. Enjoy them with your loved ones, after all, sweetness is meant to be shared!

10436064R00071